A RUBBER FACE WITH A STRIPPER'S NAME

KATJA BERG

Dear Kim,
See you at 5pm
or is it 5am?

Love

Interior Design by StandoutBooks.com

Disclaimer

This book is memoir. It reflects the author's present recollections of experiences over time. The author has tried to recreate events, locales and conversations from memory. In order to maintain their anonymity in some instances the author has changed the names of individuals and places, the author may have changed some identifying characteristics and details such as physical properties, occupations and places of residence.

The story, the experiences, and the words are the author's alone. The reader should not consider this book anything other than a work of literature.

To my beautiful children, you have taught me the value of kindness and you have inspired me to be a better person.
To my family, Mor & Far, og storesoster Taina, you have always made me feel important and have accepted me for who I am. Thank you for your support and unconditional love.
To my sisterhood and close friends, you know who you are, you have moved mountains for me.
Thank you, thank you, thank you.

Those who don't believe in magic will never find it.
– Roald Dahl, 1916–1990

CONTENTS

A Single Danish Mum and Her Conversations with Her Soul

It's my belief that redemption is a difficult thing to find in human relationships, but this should never change who we are, at our core. Losing faith in the people around us challenges us and leaves us with our backs against the wall. These lessons are often the most painful to learn, but they can bring us closer to actualising our full and complete self; the person we were truly meant to be. Carrie Fisher said, "Turn your broken heart or spirit into something you love." Carly Simon famously sang that, "There's more room in a broken heart." I took sincere inspiration and direction from these quotations, and I hope you will too. They gave me the courage to find myself again.

Dancing on the Edge

As a single mum, it's often hard enough just to get through your day-to-day routine. There are the judgements from people who barely know you (if at all), the pressure of putting food on the table, and the responsibilities you have to your kids, family, and friends. It can be hard to see the light at the end of the tunnel through this cloud of obligations, but if I can do it, the good news is that so can you. You *will* arrive on the other side; probably a bit battered and bruised, but I've yet to encounter an injury that a mimosa or two couldn't fix.

We need failure to appreciate and define success; it's an absolutely necessary part of life. The happy ending we're all chasing is part of the life that we're currently living; we just often forget that along the way. Maybe you can add your ex, the father of your kids, and your lapsed friendships, relationships, or family ties to your list of failures, but these experiences are needed – context is everything, and it's only by looking backwards that we can truly move forwards in life. We become better people when we acknowledge this. When we take ownership of our choices and where we are in life, we can figure out how to move forward and improve our lot.

This is especially true for the single mum who gets left to bring up the kids, who ends up judged in the court of public opinion for not abiding by societal norms. I was judged by those who didn't fully understand my circumstances, and maybe you have been, as well. Maybe you've faced those who tell outright lies about you, with very little consideration as to how you feel, and without any regard for the truth. Maybe you've felt shunned by your community, as if you're not good enough and don't fit in with their regime and traditions. Maybe people have chosen not to include you, just because you're a single parent. It's when families are making difficult choices, such as where to go on holiday or where to spend Christmas, that we, as single mums, are making the choices that are necessary to merely get the family through another day.

We're the ones doing the work of two people. It can be relentless and inhumane at times; running the household, carrying the shopping bags, working to pay the bills. 'Co-parenting' is a word that doesn't exist in our vocabulary, so we must play the bad cop and the good cop all at once, though in the end we're mostly just the bad cop because all we do is shout out of sheer frustration. Then there's the crippling self-doubt when other parents (in particular, other mums) judge us, telling us that what we're doing isn't right, because they have the benefit of co-parenting to fall back on. We don't have anyone to reassure us, so we start shouting at these mums, or choose to crawl away into a corner, if the weight of single-parenting has left us with no strength to stand up for ourselves.

Believe me, these individuals wouldn't judge you from behind their raised eyebrows if they knew what single mums went through every day of the week. They would instead give you a high five – after all, you deserve to feel confident that you're doing alright. I've certainly needed to hear these reassurances. I've had to remind myself that I've worked hard to do the best I could by my children, even when I arrived late at nursery and collected my kids in a rusty Nissan, even when showing up to a kid's birthday party late and forgetting the present, and even when dinner was going to be late, again, for the umpteenth time.

Many friends of mine were verbally supportive, but very few actually acted on their words. I suspect that those who didn't help or make that extra, concerted effort were really just saying it for themselves, so that once they got home for the day, they could tell themselves that they were supportive – it had nothing to do with real friendship. True friends help you move forward in life, always.

Roses Have Thorns, but Weeds Have Flowers

How does my story begin, and why did I feel compelled to put it down on paper in the first place? I had hit rock bottom and, in my darkest moments, I started writing this book. It actually started out as a diary, which my then-therapist suggested I keep. I had, for a long time, lived with anxiety and endured insomnia; every night, I would lie alone in bed, wondering how I was going to pay the next bill. By day, I was fighting my ex-partner, and by night, I was desperately trying to figure out how I could feed two kids and a dog on five pounds a day. I dreaded receiving brown envelopes; the sure sign of a debt collector, 'DO NOT IGNORE' printed on the front in red writing. They clogged up my mailbox and fed my anxiety. To this day, I still dread brown envelopes.

I watched programs such as *The Sheriffs are Coming*, *Children in Need*, and *Cowboy Builders* every day – hell, I would even record them, so that I could always get my fix. It's a sad but true fact: I needed to see that other people were worse off than me. It was a low point, I must admit, and I became that single mum who sits down in front of *Magic Mike* and prays for a sequel called *Magic*

Mike Reads a Book, just to have an excuse to watch another. I'd watch endless *Sex and the City* episodes and any other 'feel good in an instant' program or movie; anything to escape from reality, even if just for a short while. It had never been part of my plan as a mother, never something I thought I'd have to do when having a family. Then again, I never thought I'd have to deal with the fear of not surviving, either. I would order a takeaway on the expanded-to-the-limit credit card, pour a few glasses of wine, and have a small pity party for one, dancing in front of MTV's eighties hit list, much to my children's horror.

The dating scene became a challenging and exhausting afterthought – I hated asking friends to look after the kids for free, because even though they had offered help, it was never quite convenient, and I could always tell. Even when I could afford a babysitter, they'd cancel, and I'd be left slipping off my heels, knowing that I was destined for another night in, while my friends simply left the kids with their partners.

The dressing-up can be fun, but it's all the other things you have to do that leave you too tired to go out in the first place – it's like organising a school trip or a weekend away. When you combine it all, the thought of a relationship becomes crippling, because you know that you don't have the energy for it. As lonely as you feel, it's outweighed by the realisation that even considering someone else needing something from you makes you more tired.

It's the small things: not being able to just sit down and cry, take some time to yourself, or reach out to your partner to fix the printer when your deadline is looming and the kids still need to eat. The never-ending disappointment and the lack of invites to couples' dinners can haunt you, if you let it. I have discovered, however, that your true friends will decide to just have dinner parties, instead of dinners with labels attached. This includes family holidays where the word 'family' doesn't just mean Mum, Dad, and two and a half kids.

This is the reality you'll just have to deal with, as a single mum: not being able to fit in, and not because you're not an awesome girlfriend with great kids, but simply because you're working yourself to the bone, and then some, for those kids. You don't get included because there's only one of you, and for many friends, that isn't convenient. It sucks, but it is what it is, I suppose. To this day, I still haven't been invited on any holidays with friends who have partners. Maybe it's a coincidence, but at this point, I'm too seasoned to think so.

I've felt so alone, at certain points, and I mean 'alone' in the truest sense of the word. You know things are getting bad when you still feel lonely with other people in the room – in particular, at the sort of parties mentioned above. Then there's the moment when the kids have been put to bed and a sigh of relief has been exhaled, and the first glass of wine has finally been consumed. Then it hits you: there's no one to talk to or share the day with; not unless you call a friend with their own life, who might not appreciate being called every day, or your parents, who have done so much listening that your mum has gone a little deaf, totally by choice. Instead, you sit on the couch and flick through the channels, all the while missing the feeling of someone sitting next to you.

If I'd known back then that I wasn't the only one feeling this way, I'd have started this book sooner. When you go through that loneliness, when you experience the terror of tomorrow, you always feel like you're the only one. I could have shared my own troubles with lots of other single mums in the same situation, and I would have been a lot easier on myself and, ultimately, would have felt less alone.

It's been a very important learning curve for me to understand that what other people think of me is none of my business. Without coming to that realisation in full, I would have been a fragment of the person I am today.

In order to teach your kids respect, kindness, and appreciation for others and themselves, you will have to find a way to model these principles for them. Everyone has a story; it's how you allow it to be told that will shape your future.

Barbra Streisand, The Final Countdown, and Billie Holiday

❧❧❧

I was born in Frederiksberg, Copenhagen, next to the Carlsberg brewery. As a child, I got used to the smell of yeast and barley greeting me every morning. Back then, it was a rough area, but today it's one of the more fashionable places to buy a flat in Denmark. I have an older sister, Taina, who is six years older than me and named after my mum's cousin. My father was born in Denmark, with two younger sisters, and had a traditional family life. One where my grandmother stayed at home, looking after the three kids, and my grandfather worked. They were a respected family in the area of Lyngby, just outside of central Copenhagen.

My mother, Tuula, was born in Helsinki, Finland, into a family where the dynamics were completely reversed. Her father fought against Russia for nearly two years of my mum's life, so when he returned, my mum just a toddler, he felt that they couldn't connect. My mum's two younger sisters became close to him, and it made her feel disconnected from the rest of the family. He was a colourful, humorous, hard-working man, who started his own business as a mechanic. He also drank heavily and was quite volatile because of his experiences during the war. My mum was close to my grandmother, her mum, who was unable to help my mum feel more a part of the family unit, most likely due to the violent tendencies of her husband.

My mum ran away from home when she was just seventeen. She and her childhood friend, Sara, decided to travel to Cambridge, England, and then go to Denmark to settle. They wanted to establish themselves in Copenhagen and get an education. My mum suggested that they should both go and visit the family Taina (the cousin after whom my sister is named) had been with for a few years, as a child. Between 1939 and 1944, Finnish families had sent kids to Denmark, and the rest of Scandinavia, to avoid the poverty and other fallout of the horrendous Winter War. It was my father's parents, Farmor Irma and Farfar Orla, who had looked after Taina when she was younger. After the war, it had been a difficult decision for them to send her back, as she had been with them for nearly two years. Taina had kept in touch after this time, and my mum had even visited them in 1965 to pass on a gift. When the two Finnish girls visited the couple who would become my grandparents, my father, Henrik, fell for my mum instantly. He had suggested to the ladies that they could attend the same college as he did, the Rebæk Søpark College, as they rented out rooms.

My mum couldn't speak a word of Danish, so communication was a challenge. The girls only moved into the college in 1966, but love blossomed quickly between my parents. In 1967, just a year later, my sister was born, and they called her 'Taina', to celebrate the woman who had brought them together. My father studied chemistry at the University of Copenhagen, supported by his parents, while my mum got a job at Finnair Airlines, to support herself. They had each other, but their worlds were very different. Nevertheless, they moved into a small flat, where they shared a toilet with several other residents. When my sister was born, my mother could only care for her for the first three months, as this was the only maternity leave mothers were allowed to take. My father chose to study from home, which made their lives easier in terms of childcare.

My mum had started at Finnair Airlines as a ticket girl and, when she retired, she stepped down as a general account manager for Denmark. She now speaks Danish with a heavy accent, along with four other languages. Pretty incredible for a girl who ran away at seventeen and had no education! But that's no surprise, since she's an incredible, passionate person, even though she didn't have an easy introduction to the world. She was, in turn, not the easiest mum to live with; she's one of those people where, when I tell her a joke, she doesn't laugh – she doesn't respond at all, in fact. I gently tell her, "Mum, that was a joke," and she says, "I am laughing inside," before carrying on with whatever she was doing. Finnish people are hard to impress.

My father became a great scientist and was part of several large projects over the course of his career. He analysed evidence in court cases, performed forensic examinations, and assessed developments and liabilities for big companies. He's the kind of father who will, to this day, sit me down and tell me the facts of life. In a scientist's world, facts, numbers, and statistics are everything. His world is mostly black and white – no grey areas exist. My father comes from a normal, middle-class family, and my grandparents were often my saviours during the trials of my childhood, which shaped me into the person I am today. My fondest memory of them is of our trips to the Tivoli Gardens. I could bike there in fifteen minutes, down Vesterbrogade with all its little shops, and I would meet them at the gates.

All my troubles would wash away when we stepped through the gates, me holding my grandfather's hand. His grip was strong, soft, and firm, all at the same time. He would take me to the rides, and they would sit on the bench, he eating peanuts, my grandmother feeding them to the pigeons. After the rides, I would eat glazed apples with coconut flakes. It's a magical place, Tivoli, and we went several times a year, for many years. To this day, I don't have a single bad memory of my grandparents.

My grandfather wasn't the tallest man, and he had grey hair and a very round face, with an extremely warm smile. He was always dressed in linen trousers and often a pale blue shirt. This man was one of the rocks in my life. My grandmother was the tiniest woman, with white hair set by the hairdresser once a week, and glasses. She always dressed in skirts and, wherever she went, she always wore heels. She lived on black coffee and biscuits, and she was my hero. Along with my grandfather, she taught our family that family matters and comes first. They were the centre of all of our Christmas Eves, with real candles instead of fairy lights and dancing and singing in a family chain around the tree.

My childhood was fairly idyllic. At home, one night a week, we would eat Russian pancakes, which my mum cooked, and watch movies while curled up on the couch. Another night, we would be dragged around from place to place, following my parents and their friends as they partied. It was an interesting upbringing, to say the least.

I was born on the 5th of November, 1974, six years after my sister, and promptly named after my mother's Russian friend, Katja. Katja worked as a stripper at night, and with only my sister to care for, my mother agreed to look after her daughter. Once I was born, however, my mum decided they had to get a bigger place, and the arrangement had to stop. The place they bought was on the fifth floor. It was a small apartment with two bedrooms, a living room, and a balcony that looked over the Copenhagen ZOO tower on one side and the Carlsberg brewery elephant statues on the other. The Copenhagen ZOO tower was actually an owl tower built in 1885 to memorialise how animals were once kept. After her three months of maternity leave passed, my mother had my Finnish grandmother look after me for a year. Unfortunately, my grandmother had COPD, chronic obstructive pulmonary disease, a lung disease that makes it harder and harder to breathe, which started affecting her in a profound way, and living on the fifth floor with no lift was a problem. Eventually, she had to return to Finland. I was really grateful that my grandmother had looked after me. We shared a bond that I didn't have with my mother's father. My mother's relationship with her father was tense until his death, even though she was the one always making sure he could come to visit her and his other two daughters, who had also moved to Denmark. My grandmother died when I was around six years old, and my grandfather and I spoke less and less, until he eventually died when I was thirty years old.

When my grandmother left to go back to Finland, my parents got hold of a nanny, who was a friend from my mum's Finnish circle. Her name was Hannah, and to this day, I remember her smell, her manners, and her unconditional love for me. She had a daughter, Pia, who was three years older than me, and we became close friends, even after Hannah stopped being my nanny. When I was about nine years old, Hannah died suddenly of organ failure, due to heavy drinking, and Pia and her little brother, Henry, had to go back to Finland, where their estranged father lived. I lost two very important people over a very short time in my life, and I still remember the sting of loss.

I was a peculiar child – quiet and imaginative. I could spend hours pretending I was in another world. I would drag a hair dryer around, singing into the plug as if it was a microphone, and would walk and dance around with my ballerina dress over my swimsuit, wearing two different shoes. I was quite strange-looking, with an underbite and braces on both my upper and lower teeth that pulled my chin back. My ears stuck out, I had big, round cheeks, and my auntie Ulla, my dad's youngest sister, used to cut my hair to save money, leaving me with a classic bowl cut. On top of all that, I had to sleep wearing a helmet that the dentist promised would correct my underbite, leaving me with morning bedhead that I usually struggled to correct. I always looked really dirty, as I enjoyed playing in the field with the boys, rather than indoors with the girls. This led to my dad giving me the nickname 'Roskis', which means 'bin' in Finnish or 'Gummi fjaes' which was 'rubberface' in Danish. I had tomboyish manners and always made funny faces at people.

My crutch was my dog, Laura, who was a St. Bernard/Collie mix. She was my rock when I felt alone, my confidant, and my comfort when I needed it. My parents had gotten her at almost the same time they'd bought the new flat, so I wasn't even one year old when she was a puppy, and she often slept in the same bed as me.

My parents loved me and my sister unconditionally, but I never saw them much as they worked a lot. They also socialised a lot and partied, but it was the norm in the seventies, and I don't blame them. It probably made me more independent and helped me become the woman I am today. We travelled a lot, with my mum's work, on short and cheap holidays – we would get what we called 'standby tickets' and, because our school wasn't strict with regards to taking time off, we would frequently see other cultures. Despite all the partying, my sister and I got to visit China, South Africa, and several European nations – we spent every summer in Finland, where we had friends with summer houses or cabins, or in France, where my parents, a few years later, bought a house for the summer holidays. We were lucky in that sense. We were at one point called the 'Holiday Inn Daughters', as we stayed in Holiday Inn hotels so often. To this day, I'm more of a hotel girl than a camper lady – I'd happily relinquish tents and caravans for a minibar and a bathrobe.

Denmark was a great place to be a kid, but the culture was often intrusive. Denmark was so liberal that, in my opinion, too much got thrown at kids. You would have Danish series and movies showing tits or sex, no matter what time of day it was, and as a result, I consumed many things that I should not have seen or heard as a young child. The parties were hippie-like, and everyone had their tits out at the beach, with a very strong "It's natural!" attitude as a defence. It felt, at times, like I was living in an open community without having chosen to do so. That said, I do miss the lack of judgment between parents in those times. Now, when a parent smokes a cigarette on a playground, they could easily be lynched, when in reality, they're just there to watch their kids play – and if they're outside, they're not on their phones! We could also do with more chatting between parents nowadays. When I was a child, parents had no phones, so they would get to know each other while their children played.

When I was three years old, I went to what we in Denmark call 'kindergarten' – a government program that helps parents go back to full-time work at very little monthly cost. In kindergarten, I remember being a really active kid. Everyone used bicycles to get to work or to drop the kids off at nursery, and it was only a short ride from our home. The kindergarten was a small building, but it had a playground and lots of trees to climb. In those days, kids were allowed to climb trees. My friend Bente and I would giggle a lot. Once, we couldn't stop giggling and, after many attempts to stop us, the kindergarten teacher sat us down. She'd had enough, so she placed a washing peg on each of our mouths, making sure we stayed quiet. Of course, this made us laugh even more, and the pegs flew up in the air with a snap. When my mum came to collect me, I was sitting on a table with a peg squeezing my lips together. There were bruises around my mouth. Bente was in a separate room and, at this stage, we no longer found it funny. My parents were furious, and the teacher's behaviour was eventually addressed, but it was an indication of how things were then; the so-called 'open learning' everyone was raving about was failing miserably. On my last day of kindergarten, we brought in ice cream and goodie bags for everyone. The teachers announced that I should have brought paper plates, as it was inconvenient for them to clean it all up. Considering they had a dinner lady doing this, the comment was again a reminder that we, as kids, were annoying to look after and disturbed their time as adults.

When I was five years old, I started attending Rahbekskolen School, which was again just walking distance from the flat my parents had bought in Frederiksberg. The surroundings were green, with quiet roads, despite being in the middle of the city. I remember, on my first day of school, holding my father's hand and walking down the road, with my new bright blue book bag, which had a train on the front. My hair looked like Prince Valiant's, and I was wearing a velvet tracksuit with trumpet-shaped legs, which I had inherited from my big sister. We were walking down a little alleyway, and the smell of yeast was heavy in the air. The Carlsberg brewery would become an annual school trip destination. At the end of the tours each year, teachers got free beers, and we'd get samples of Carlsberg's sodas. It was pretty obvious why we kept going back.

I was so excited to meet my class that I skipped all the way. At that age, I wasn't shy at all, and when I look back at pictures from that time, I feel I was a little too brave, considering how ridiculous I looked! Those were the days of being oblivious to how much looks mattered. My dress sense was dictated by what my sister handed down to me – my parents really didn't think that what people wore was important. They were quite relaxed about things like fashion, and looking smart was, for them, all about being practical and comfortable.

The Danish school system in the eighties and nineties was very different from today's school systems, and was miles away from the English school system. There were (and still are) no uniform policies, and the whole system was extremely down to Earth. Looking back, it was perhaps a little too laid back. It was the hippie community, and in particular the left-leaning, liberal types, who became teachers. My school was full of velvet, high-waisted, trumpet-shaped trousers that sat tight around the arse. Bras were abandoned, punk music was played loud and proud, and smoking was permitted everywhere, including at school. Often, when you knocked on the staff room door, you could hear the music. If you peeked in, you could see the cigarette smoke inside. If it was later on in the day, particularly if it was a Friday, there would always be some wine or beer on the tables. Everyone had long hair, both the men and women, and everyone's attitude was, "If it's part of life, there's no need to hide it."

The school had three levels, with the younger classes at the top and the older classes at the bottom. Each class only had about fifteen students, and the building had two gyms and a paved back yard, into which we were thrown between classes, in the interest of fresh air. We had the same Danish teacher, Inger, throughout our nine years in school, and we soon developed a great relation-ship. She saw us grow into people; 'small adults', as she always said. We would have her for Danish lessons and religion classes, and she would be the one who organised trips, weekly events, and parents' evenings. We also had a maths teacher, English teacher, German teacher, and biology teacher for a few hours every week. I particularly remember my carpentry teacher, Peter. Every Friday, at midday, he would have us bang nails into planks of wood and use drilling machines on our own, while he went and had a few beers in his office with a colleague who had also left his students. The lesson was two hours long, and Peter would come back in the last half-hour. We'd all see he was quite tipsy, and he'd smell of beer. We knew, too, that he would correct our work if needed, so it would look like he'd taught us for both hours of the lesson. I'm not sure how responsible it was, to be honest, but I remember we had fun – besides, we didn't know any better. It never dawned on us to say anything, as we had loads of fun with the drilling machines, hammers, screwdrivers, and other tools.

I got good grades in English, as it was one of the few subjects that actually held my interest. This was primarily due to my parents having a family friend move in for a year, when I was about nine years old, because of some money problems. He was from Cambridge, and he helped teach me to speak English. English came more easily to me because of his involvement. As I had recently started horse riding (which became quite a big passion of mine), he pulled his weight by taking me out, walking Laura, teaching me English, and keeping the house clean.

At the time, all the parents who were attending parent-teacher evenings, or school performances, would go with the teachers to have a few pints down at the pub. On one of these evenings, my parents were asked to wait until the end of the meeting, to speak with the teacher. They sat down, and the teacher explained how she was worried about me and the language I chose to use at school. At that time, I was very defensive about what I felt was right and wrong. If there was too much homework assigned, or I felt that some other perceived injustice was taking place, I would swear a lot.

My dad looked at my teacher and said, "It's her mother's fault. She has a very strong accent and can't correct our daughter in her pronunciation."

My mother was mortified and, that night, my dad took me home while my mum went to the pub with the teachers. The subject for that night would be my dad, not my choice of language.

Parents and teachers had a friendlier relationship at that time, and it was much more relaxed than it is now. There was no judgement – instead, there was a sense of community. We stuck together and were grateful for each other. Mothers didn't attack teachers, as they do nowadays. On the other hand, teachers allowed the kids to sit on the pavement to have lunch, even when it was sunny outside, and they never considered all the bugs the kids might have eaten. "It's all protein," they said. Teachers were less judgemental too – they didn't consider letting six-year-old kids have a night off as the mark of a terrible mother.

I developed into quite a free-spirited wild child. I listened to Billie Holiday, Barbra Streisand, and other popular sixties music. I could, at my aunt's family parties, sit for hours listening to her collection of vinyl records. Later, it was *The Final Countdown*, by the Swedish band Europe, that inspired me to have my perm cut into a mullet. This, combined with my facial features and braces, made me quite the eyesore, but it did grant me some freedom from not having to be pretty, and I could act as the class clown without being heckled for it. From the age of eleven, it started becoming noticeable that I wasn't particularly pretty, and 'Rubber Face' became my nickname with everyone, not just my dad. Even though I was always an independent and funny kid, it did start getting to me, even as I relished the space it gave me and the expectations it overturned. My friends would have beautiful hairdos and clothes that matched, but I was just Rubber Face.

I loved my horse riding and had started to cycle on my own – it became a form of escapism. I went almost every day after school, until I was twelve, which was when my interests began to change. School was still fine – I was still a tomboy with a quirky look, but while I acted tough, I often felt insecure when challenged. My parents hit a wall and, sadly, separated around this time. They had argued for a long time and, on some evenings, I would have no idea where my father had gone, or why my mother hadn't come home yet. The loneliness hardened me into a resilient person. My sister had turned eighteen and was sharing a flat with our cousin, so she was out of the picture. She was at an age where she could not, and did not, want to deal with adult issues, so I suffered alone. My grandparents and my auntie, my hair dresser, were the only ones I talked to.

When I couldn't cope, I would escape down to Vesterbro. This was the next borough, which was only a few blocks away, and where the bad boys spent their free time. I was attracted to streetwise types and felt I could connect with these delinquents. Something about their attitude struck a chord; you only had yourself, so you might as well get on with it. Looking back, I realise they were probably just kids feeling a little lost, the same as I was. My parents would have been worried sick if they'd known, but because they had so many problems, in addition to me being the quiet child, they never really knew what I was up to. They were too consumed by their impending separation, the related arguments, and the accusations to bother asking.

My parents were separated for a year, and it was messy, to say the least. I remember how the feeling of going to my dad's new flat every second weekend was a reminder of our broken home. There was no room for me; it was, after all, solely my father's flat, occupied only by his desk, where he worked all the time and smoked. The constant tapping of his computer keyboard and the smoke from his cigarettes made me run down to my auntie, who lived in the same building. I spent a lot of time there, and sometimes even slept there, as I felt more at home and attended to. At my mum's place, I had my dog and my friends nearby, but she was more concerned with talking about the divorce, drinking wine with her friends, and working all hours. At nearly thirteen, I was cooking for myself, walking the dog, and looking after myself completely. I was angry, and I got even more angry when, a year later, I realised that my parents were getting back together. Now they suddenly had an opinion on what I was doing and where I was. Even worse, after all the shit they'd put me through, they were all loving and caring and, out of nowhere, expected me to just forget all the incidents and arguments, all the pain I had experienced. I remembered sitting in my room, listening to the shouting of my father saying how much he hated my mum, and my mother saying she hoped he would move out fast. They were both drunk. It was like that almost every night, for many months. After a while, it ate into my soul. I would sit on the floor, hugging my legs while rocking back and forth, wondering why they didn't think about me upstairs, able to hear every word of it. Now, all of a sudden, they wanted me to be a kid again.

After they got back together, I became even more independent and disinterested in what my parents had to say. Becoming a teenager, I was dealing with a myriad of new hormones and emotions, and this cocktail made for a wild time to come. You could say this was when my screaming started.

My parents were back together, and I got through Rahbekskolen. I was fourteen when I graduated from year nine and went on to what is similar to an English business college. I studied business, marketing, and economics in English. It was interesting, but I was more interested in partying until the early morning. My memories of those years are hazy, to say the least. My parents had realised I was going to do my own thing, and I was too independent for them to tell me what to do. I remember my fellow students and I would often crash at someone's house after a night of heavy drinking. We'd borrow new clothes and drive into college in the morning. Quite often, we had to stop so that someone could open the car door and puke!

I got through it, though – I didn't have the best grades, but I'd already accepted that Taina was the academic one. My goal was just to get through it, and I made some amazing friends and stayed in touch with many of them after we finished school. I was a popular kid, and this always came down to the fact that I didn't take myself too seriously. I had stayed with the philosophy that it was easier to let the other girls be the pretty ones; I would much rather be the funny one. That way I was protected from being rejected. I had no boyfriend, but a lot of my friends were boys. I had kissed a few boys when alcohol had been involved, but I was a virgin until I left for England. This was quite unusual, in my circle of friends – most of them had lost their virginities at about fourteen or fifteen. It was almost a competition between the girls. I was one of only two girls left in the group who were still intact, and we had a bet that the first one to lose it had to buy the other a case of beer.

One day, we were all sitting in a friend's flat after school, when my friend, Danielle, walked in with her legs in an almost squat position. She was carrying a case of beer! Well, everyone started cheering – it was almost like a girls' frat house. It was official: I was the last one to go all the way. Most of my friends were these beautiful Scandinavian girls with perfect noses, long hair, flat stomachs, and long legs. I was the absolute opposite, until I turned sixteen. Boys would kiss me and fumble, but they didn't take it further.

Slowly, I started blossoming. I had my ears corrected by a private doctor, against my parents' wishes – if I had looked like a monkey's arse, they still wouldn't have cared. Most parents tend to think their kid is the most beautiful thing in their lives, so I didn't listen to them. My braces came off, and I started to dye my hair and follow fashion.

One day, I was asked to sit as a makeup and hair model by one of my friends from college who had flunked out and started studying to be a makeup artist. She got the pictures published and, after that, I started being offered work as a face model. Although I still had the feeling of not being pretty, the experience gave me some confidence. I had my picture on the front of a hair-dressers' magazine and was signed up to an agency called 'Special Models' on an amateur basis. Still, I would get completely confused when a guy approached me, thinking he wanted my girl-friend's number when he actually wanted mine. While totally missing this, I'd blurt out a bad joke and give no number at all, and he would walk away, not very amused. I still had my Rubber Face nickname, but it had less meaning now.

When I was seventeen, I graduated from business college and started working in several different bars around town. In Denmark, these tend to close at about five in the morning, so I was almost working full-time. Danielle bought a flat, and I moved in with her. Those were wild and great times. She eventually decided to go to America for a year and rented her room out to a mutual friend called Tanja, who was even wilder, and we had a life of partying and working hard in bars. When Danielle returned from America, I decided to go to London. I was nearly nineteen years old and in need of something new in my life.

Bring It On

L ike everyone else, I fell in love with London as soon as I
arrived. I had arranged to live in a Danish Christian
YMCA, which was run by a Danish priest. The YMCA was
located in Hampstead, one of the most beautiful areas in North
London. It reminded me a lot of Copenhagen; the green grass,
beautiful houses, and sheer compactness of the town helped
combat my homesickness. The weekly rent was fifty pounds and
this included breakfast. We were four girls in one room, all in
bunk beds. Two of the girls were friends from home and had
come to London together. They were from an area of Copenhagen I was quite familiar with, and we clicked immediately, especially because we were all out of work and ready to run through
our savings before trying to find a job. The adrenaline of being in
London alone was thrilling. Because the YMCA was run by a
priest, we had to crawl in and out of windows when coming back
late, as the doors closed at eleven, and no keys were given out.
You would arrange who was going to let you back in with the ones
who weren't going out, with the promise that you'd do the same
for them later on. The YMCA staff would check the windows
before bed time, so when we were home late, we would call the

person inside, and they would come and open a window on the lower ground. Trying to open the door from inside meant you had to pass the priest's room – if he was awake and caught you, you could lose your bunk.

I met some beautiful people in London, both Danish and English. It was great to have my new Danish friends to remind me of home while I familiarised myself with this new world. Finally, I got some work at the RAF club on Piccadilly Lane. I started as a waitress and worked split shifts. It was Camilla, one of the Danish girls from the YMCA, who got me the job. After a while, I was asked to move in as a live-in member of staff. It was appealing, and I made friends with many more English people as I became more established.

At work, I wore white lace aprons over pinstriped suits in pinks and burgundies, with tall lace collars. I looked like a 'lagkage' – a traditional, multi-layered, Danish cake served at birthdays. I was serving kippers at breakfast time, and learned quickly to call the RAF members 'sir' and 'lady'. Later, I got moved down to what they called 'the Buttery', where I served lemon chicken and had to do the odd melba toast in the kitchen. These were slices of toast for a luxury pâté that was served in the restaurants, and I was often asked to make them when the manager had had enough of my sly jokes about the uniforms and the sirs and ladies. He wasn't impressed, and many times my liberal upbringing clashed with the very conservative English norms of the time.

Slowly but surely, I began to create a life for myself in London. My parents came to visit over a few short weekends, and we stayed in close touch. I started dating a chef, Miguel, who was eight years older than me, and finally became an adult in a sexual sense. The relationship didn't work out, and I was heartbroken for a while. I left the RAF club and rented a flat with Camilla, after which I started to look for jobs in Soho. I was twenty years old when I got a job on Old Compton Street, in a French restaurant with a predominantly gay clientele. We served many vibrant theatre people, which was right up my alley. It was here I met my first love, Draco. He was half-Greek, half-English, and came from Chigwell, in Essex, which was the last stop on the Central Line, and where *Birds of a Feather* was shot. He had a cockney accent and was absolutely stunning. When I met him, he was planning to travel the world, and I was definitely not part of this plan. In my defence, he wasn't part of mine, either.

We worked together and soon started a casual relationship, telling each other that we were just spending time together for fun. He came to Denmark to visit my family and friends, and I met all his friends and family. We became deeply involved in each other's lives. His departure was approaching, and we soon realised that we'd been kidding ourselves the entire time. I was so in love with him that I couldn't spend a night away from him. He spent most of the week with me, and the thought of us not being able to see each other made me suggest that I could join him on his travels, to which he agreed. He'd been too afraid to ask me to give everything up for him; he told me that he wanted me to do it for me. I could work for three months in Denmark, if I was to go back, via a system where you could use all your tax relief for the year, and then I would have enough to go to Australia and meet him there. My whole world became about Draco. His friend, Chris, who he was planning on travelling with, wasn't impressed, worrying that he would have to cut his travels short.

The day arrived, and he left. For those first couple of weeks, I sobbed nearly every day. I quit my job, left my flat, and said goodbye to my friends without ever doubting my decision to go and meet my love in Australia. I went back to live with my parents in Copenhagen and slept on the couch. I soon got a job in the Copenhagen airport, serving Danish open sandwiches in yet another pinstriped uniform. I spoke to Draco on the phone several times a week, which made me even more determined to soldier on and save as much money as I could. Toby, a friend of

Draco's, wanted to go to Oz too, and we agreed to travel together.

Our day of departure finally arrived, and a friend of my mum's arranged cheap airfare for us. I was so excited and couldn't wait to go. When we reached the airport, my mum cried – it was the first time she'd ever broken down in front of me, especially *because* of me. She just sobbed into my shoulder. My father was always an emotional mess, so I was used to him crying, but my mother? I was almost in shock and didn't know how to handle it. It seemed a little late for my parents to be worried about me. I had been on my own for so long that their concern felt more confusing than anything else. I loved them, but I was a loner. I did things on my own and in my own way.

After a thirty-six hour flight, Toby and I landed in Sydney. I was jetlagged and almost trembling at passport control – I desperately wanted to see the love of my life. We came out, and there he was. Draco waved and gave me a huge hug and a kiss on the cheek. I was so confused; it was more like meeting a friend. In fact, Draco and Chris seemed more excited to see Toby, and I stood there in the outfit I'd agonised over, my hair specially prepared and my pocket full of hard-earned money. I'd travelled to the other side of the planet to meet him, and I got a hug – a fucking hug.

They'd sorted a hostel out, and so we all went there. The hostel was a building smack in the middle of Sydney, with twenty rooms all containing bunkbeds. All rooms shared one kitchen with two fridges, a terrace, and a dining area. There were washing lines across each room, even in the kitchen, and everyone stooped over to do their washing and to have a shower before moving on. Draco was almost avoiding me, and so I decided to get drunk. I was in Sydney with only a backpack and had no idea if the man I was madly in love with was even happy to see me. I got drunk, ignored him, and spoke to anyone who wasn't him. I was talking to a few backpackers when he suddenly walked in, pulled me out of the room, and kissed me in the hallway. He said nothing, instead leading me down to our room. He went to the terrace and sat me down, taking a deep breath. My heart was pounding, and I was about to cry – my head was spinning from the combination of booze and jetlag.

"I love you, Kat," he said. "I'm just so afraid that you're here because of me and not for your own reasons. I want you to be here, and I don't want this feeling to go away." I looked at him, waiting for the 'but...', and he continued. "But I want to travel and see more of the world. I just can't take the chance of losing you, either. I'm so in love with you, so I'm confused, and I'm sorry that my behaviour has been cold since you arrived, but it's stirred up a lot of feelings in me. I can see you're here more because of me than actually seeing the world, and I'm realising that I'm not sure if I feel the same way."

I looked at him, and I suddenly realised that he'd moved away from me both physically and emotionally. Travel had become his number one priority, and upon finally seeing me, he felt that he owed me an apology, or at the very least, the bravery to say that he regretted his choice.

"Draco," I said, "I've always wanted to see Australia and go backpacking. Let's just see where this goes, shall we? And I love you, too."

He grabbed me, and we made love and fell asleep in each other's arms, not even caring if anyone else was in the room. I fell asleep to the sound of the love of my life snoring, knowing I had just told him the biggest lie. I hated the whole idea of backpacking and the idea of lying in tents in Australia. I'd read a book about the ten most dangerous animals in the world before my departure, and to my pleasant surprise, they all lived in Australia. I knew this was the beginning of the end. My heart was breaking, but my mind kept telling me to just enjoy it while it lasted.

After five months, the relationship finally crumbled under its own weight. I couldn't keep pretending that I loved the caravans when I was scared every night that spiders and snakes would climb in and surprise me in my sleeping bag. I had called my mum and told her that I wanted to come home. My parents were there when I needed them, and their response began a renewed, stronger relationship between us. My mum organised tickets home for me, and I found myself with a week left in Oz. Draco and I decided to go to an island surrounded by blue jellyfish (just my luck!), meaning we couldn't swim, but we enjoyed each other regardless. We didn't speak much, because I was deflated that he'd chosen the travelling after everything I'd given up for him, but I knew that fighting it wouldn't help. I knew it was over. He was trying to make it better and gave me lots of attention. We had such a deep connection, and he gave it up to travel the world. I had to admit to him that I had lied that night in the hostel, and I didn't like travelling as a backpacker and working on chestnut-picking farms – between wood spiders and all the other creepy crawlies, I was just here for him. I wasn't sure whether to hate him or just love him for as long as I could. My survival mode kicked in, and I resolved to just keep going forward. I was done talking, and loving him seemed easier than hating him.

A week later, I was leaving. Chris and Toby arranged a farewell party, and Draco was in turmoil, but he seemed adamant, at the end of the day, that it was the right decision. We drank and spoke a lot, and since everyone was in great spirits, I pretended I was, as well. I played the strong Kat, as usual, and told everyone we had made the right decision, knowing inside that it had been his choice entirely; I had wanted him to make the choice to come home with me. I flew to Seoul and caught a connecting flight to France, where my parents were holidaying, crying for thirty-six hours straight. I sat squeezed between several Koreans, who were washing their feet using airline towels, smiling and laughing at me while speaking Korean. Maybe they were trying to encourage me not to cry – after all, nothing could be that bad. Perhaps they were laughing at the fact that my face was so swollen from crying that it looked like I'd had an allergic reaction to something. My father had organised a cab to collect me, and the cab driver kept speaking to me in French, which soothed me a little. When I arrived at the house, the warmth and the smell of French food made me feel at home. My parents' house was in a small village in the south of France, and their neighbours knew I was coming. They waved from their windows, shouting, "Bonsoir, mademoiselle!" and all I did was look up and cry. My dad ran to me, picked up my suitcase, and pulled me into the house.

My parents hugged me and fed me, and my mum said, "If he loved you, he wouldn't have let you go."

I learned to accept this, and it has been a mantra for me, ever since. If a real man truly loves you, he won't let you go.

I Love Me, I Love Me Not

❧❀❧

A week went by, and all I did was sleep, cry, eat French food, and drink lots of wine. Some people might say, "What was there to cry about?", but it was the first time I'd truly had my heart broken. It was the kind of heartbreak where you wake up and, for a few seconds, everything feels fine – then you remember what has happened, and a deep pain springs up suddenly in your heart, and it feels like something is physically breaking anew. This was when I truly started believing that you could die of a broken heart.

Wherever my parents took me, I sat like a robot, eating the food in front of me and listening to my parents tell me that I could do better. Deep inside, I knew they were just relieved that I'd come back. I can appreciate that fact now, because I have kids myself, but back then, I just felt that they were being selfish and didn't understand me at all.

Eventually, we returned to Denmark. My parents needed to go back to work, and I had to start earning some money. When I returned to Copenhagen, I found work almost immediately in a couple of bars. I would come home late at night, or early in the morning; often, I'd arrive home to see my father's bedroom light on through the crack beneath his door. He would actually lie awake until I got home safe. It was very different to what I was used to, but it was endearing.

My parents decided to sell the flat I had grown up in. The area had become extremely popular, and the housing market was going through a massive boom at the time, so it was an opportunity they couldn't pass up. My mother took an early retirement after working at Finnair for thirty-six years, and my father was working as a freelancer for several forensic companies and private clients.

With the sale, they could buy a property in Osterbro, a luxurious area, not far from the flat, a place where all the tourists went to see one of Copenhagen's major attractions, the Little Mermaid statue. The iconic statue was modelled after the character from Hans Christian Andersen's story of the same name about a mermaid who would give up her soul, sea life, and identity to be a human. It was situated by the harbour, which was just a stone's throw away from the new property my parents bought.

There were three flats: one for me, one for my sister, and my parents kept the middle one for when they came to the city, as they had decided to spend the rest of the money on a beach house on the north coast. They got the best of both worlds, and they truly spoiled me and my sister.

I moved in and swiftly lost myself in a haze of working, partying, and paying the bills. Draco faded away – it was a case of 'out of sight, out of mind'. I started creating a wall around myself – I wasn't prepared to have my heart broken again. I dated many guys, but I would order a cab the next day and, if they were lucky, they would get a cup of tea or coffee. When crashing at their places, I would just leave. I never looked back.

When I had just turned twenty-three, I became bored with working in bars and got a small job at my friend Vanessa's flower shop, which was located in the middle of Copenhagen. Despite being a small shop, it was very well-established and catered to a high-class clientele. I learned to create flower arrangements from scratch, swept the floors, made coffee, and went with Vanessa to the markets. I learned how to put colours together, to follow my creative instincts and go with the flow. Soon, I was creating designs using plants and fresh-cut flowers with an artistry not expected of a florist. I researched Tage Andersen, whose floristry was influenced by the art exhibitions he hosted in his shop. He is a sculptor, artist, and overall Renaissance man. Then there was the florist Erik Bering. He was the supplier to the queen of Denmark and created flowers for clubs, bars, and huge events in London. We were often asked to do work for him, or deliver to him.

It was exhilarating to find something that really made me happy, and I often dreamt about going back to London to work as a florist, as England was still under my skin. I had been in contact with both my Danish and English friends, and they had all tried to persuade me to come back. After two years working with flowers, I decided to rent out the flat in Copenhagen, which was owned by my parents anyway, and move back to London.

I had reconsidered my whole career and living situation, and I started thinking about opening my own business. I'd been saving money for a long time and wanted to invest it in a project of my own, for a change. I threw myself a huge going away party. The reasoning behind my leaving was, to many people, mind-blowing. Financially, I was in a good place. I'd saved a lot and, because I was renting out the flat, I left with no bills to pay, and had even made a small profit.

I'd always been a fish out of water in Denmark. Even with a beautiful flat in Copenhagen, a brilliant job in the city, and great friends around me, I couldn't wait to go back and live in a rented room with carpet on the bathroom floors, risking all my hard-earned money on a business I didn't even know how to start.

When I arrived, I stayed with my good friend Daniel who I'd met at the RAF club during my first visit to London. He lived in

Fulham, on Sherbrooke Road, and worked in the pub directly underneath his flat. I started working in Fulham, at a florist called Dansk Flowers, which was just around the corner, on Wandsworth Road. The owner had started his business as a stall under the Danish Embassy, and the name had stuck. The manager was Danish and a typical Scandinavian woman – tall, long-legged, with a beautiful face, and she was hard-working too. It was almost like being at home, and I settled in quickly. I planned to learn a lot about the flower styles in England and the English way of selling flowers; everything from the wrapping to the colours. Even the names of the flowers were a whole new world to me.

It was here that I met Polly, who would become my confidante and best friend. She was also a florist in the making. Polly is a Fulham girl, and she knows every corner and person in Fulham. She was brought up just off King's Road, in a small house, with two sisters and a brother. She was a petite girl with a dashing taste in clothes, and I often told her that she looked like Mariah Carey, with her long blonde hair and sweeping fringe. She hadn't had an easy upbringing, but she had such a positive outlook on life regardless, and that impressed me immensely.

We became close and often went to the theatre together. We watched Shakespeare plays, including the time we got to see Joseph Fiennes in a production of the classic comedy *Love's Labour's Lost*, as well as a few different productions of *Hamlet*. Right afterwards, we would hit the bars, where we would meet her tall, ginger-haired boyfriend, Chey. Chey, who had his roots in Ireland and whose whole family were living in Fulham, instantly became a friend. For many years, I didn't understand a word he said to me because of the accent. He didn't worry too much and told me that at least I couldn't argue with what I didn't understand. I suppose that's every man's dream.

I still played hard and worked hard. I started researching shop leaseholds, but understood nothing. I also researched areas and went many times to Hampstead Heath, where I'd originally started off in England. I felt nothing; I wasn't thrilled, and I found that I had to look somewhere else completely.

Friends told me that the south-western areas were pretty, and Polly and I took the district line to Richmond upon Thames. I walked out of the train station and, after a few minutes, I turned to Polly and said, "This is it." My whole body was trembling – I was in love. The small-town feeling, the narrow alleyways, the beautiful buildings, the decorative pubs, the independent shops... it was just so gorgeous. It was also liberating to see that people still cared about individuality in design.

We searched for hours, until I eventually found the estate agent who dealt with most shop leases in the area. After a few more trips to Richmond, the agent phoned to tell me that a shop was available, and I went to see it with a friend. It was huge. The front of the shop was comprised of old, white tiles from the '50s, and I already wanted to paint it bright red. Walking through the old shop door, with an old-school style bell ringing whenever someone entered, was simply exhilarating. The shop window was the same size as a whole side wall of the shop, and my first vision was of a display of flowers that told the fairy tales of Han Christian Andersen. There was a back room, where storage and a small office would fit nicely, and a small outside area in the back, where I would keep the flower bins. Polly and I went to a local bar and, over some vodka, decided it was the shop for me. I went home to sleep it off, happy as I collapsed into bed. My dream of being an independent shop owner, and creating my own designs in London, was nearly a reality. The next day, I called a local lawyer in Richmond, who helped me set the deal up and finally explained to me what a leasehold was. I resigned from my job and found a new place in Ealing for myself, as I needed to be closer to Richmond and not tempted to party so frequently. The place was almost as cheap as my previous flat, with pink carpets, an electric fire (the type that kills you in your sleep), and the classic Chinese restaurant just underneath. I looked forward to the scent of fried food and the drunk people on Friday nights keeping me awake. I loved it. This was the beginning of a hectic, beautiful time in my life – these were the best and the most challenging years I have ever been through, even with everything that was to come afterwards.

The owner of the shop was a Turkish family man who had worked his whole life and had two daughters and a son. The son owned the dry cleaner's next door, and one daughter was still at home, living with him and his wife and being a mother at the age of thirty-three. His other daughter had moved out and had established her own family. He was a kind man, and he would visit the shop many times throughout the years.

The shop agreement came through, and my parents came over and helped me paint the walls, remove the carpets, and put shelves up. Everything was bought used or had been recycled, as I had no money to buy anything new. We worked day and night, and my parents were extremely supportive. I didn't even have a till, but I did hire an accountant, who advised me on margins, daily sales targets, book keeping, etc.

Toby, who I had travelled with in Australia, came back after nearly two years of travelling with Draco. He settled in Brighton, where he was originally from, and used me as a guinea pig in his burgeoning career as a graphic designer, creating an incredibly beautiful logo that I could use on business cards. A year after my arrival in London, I still hadn't been in contact with Draco, and I never asked Toby about him, either – I knew he was living with someone else, and I had put my broken heart behind me and focused on creating something beautiful, instead. In Denmark, we have a saying: 'If the fireworks didn't go off properly, you should never walk back, as they might blow up in your face.' This was the attitude I had with Draco. This was my moment, and mine alone.

Starting the business was absolutely crazy. Terms like 'leasehold', 'break clause', 'public liability insurance', 'business rates',

'P60', 'corporation tax', 'VAT payments', etc. soon took a toll on me, as I quickly realised that I had bitten off more than I could chew. It was tough finding a supplier as, since I was a woman, foreign, and new to the flower business in London, many of them tried to hustle me. My work experience in Copenhagen helped me see through their attempts, but it was tiring, trying to compete in a man's world.

I painted the shopfront red and added its new name to the front door, in gold letters: 'Roseberg Flowers of Copenhagen'. Walking into the shop, I had realised there were tiles that had been hidden under the carpet when I took over the shop, and they were now on display. The shelves were made of old wood and filled with pots and vases imported from Denmark and Belgium. The plants were from Danish suppliers, and they were just like the ones I had been brought up with, "Dronning Ingrid", was the pale pink pelargonie named after our queen in Denmark. I had bought an old street lamp, which I placed in front of the shop, and I began to arrange old champagne buckets full of fresh posies under the gazebo, each morning. Everyone who passed stopped and enjoyed the floral painting, which would greet them on their way to work, the train station, or shopping.

I bought fresh-cut flowers from markets in London, and also directly from the competitive markets in surrounding areas. I had access to the 'Dutch flower trucks', which delivered straight to the shop, and somehow I made it through the first year and kept things running – not always smoothly, particularly to begin with, but running nonetheless. I'd spent a lot of time networking, too. It was a real case of blood, sweat, and tears.

Slowly but surely, I began to build a reputation, and soon I was known as a real florist, specialising in events and weddings. I created bouquets for the dinner parties of rich bankers and famous people living on the hill. Although business was picking up, I was still filing losses due to the business's difficult conception, but I was heading in the right direction. I would go to the market, open the shop, organise the flowers, serve all day and, in the evening, do my book-keeping or arrange the next day's deliveries. It was a seven-day-a-week job, and I loved every minute of it.

My parents often visited and, on one of the many days my father had been in the shop to help me sweep and cut flowers, he said, "You could sell ice to Eskimos." I think he felt sorry for the men who came into my shop, often just to look, and instead ended up leaving with some decadent floral creation.

Madness on Toast

After spending a year and a half running the shop and
developing the business, things finally started to take
shape. However, maintaining things at that relentless pace was
hard, and it began to take its toll. I had chronic headaches and
was so tired that I couldn't sleep at all. Working one hundred
hours per week had paid off, but I realised that I couldn't carry on
like this. Finally, I came to the conclusion that I needed someone
to work for me, even if only for a few days a week. I had a few
different Sunday girls, and my friend, Sam, who I had met
through the shop, had a fifteen-year-old daughter, Sienna, who
came in to help every Saturday. The help gave me some relief and
much-needed time to think up some new ideas, attend
networking events, and occasionally get out to see my friends,
who were still partying hard. I was more sensible than I had been
for ages. The bank account had a lot to do with it, but there was
also the fact that when you own your own business, you can't call
in sick.

One morning, a new delivery man came in with some flowers
from my suppliers. I remember how, when he walked in, my jaw

dropped straight to the floor. I knew I was going to be with this man. He looked like a tall, dark-haired Jason Statham. He was strong and handsome, had a beautiful smile with dimples, and the attraction between us was palpable. I was almost speechless and fumbled some words about him sounding very English when he told me he was of Dutch ancestry – not really the best chat-up line. He was very charming, but also rather shy. After he left, I phoned my sister and told her that I wanted to marry this man. I babbled on about how gorgeous he was – I must have sounded completely flustered. She probably thought I had finally lost the plot.

His name was Casper. He started coming to the shop more regularly, and we started chatting, with things slowly evolving from there. When I first met him, he was in a relationship. I had never had an affair with anyone and didn't want to start now. He started helping me close the shop, and we went for a drink together at a few local pubs. It became very clear that we were attracted to one another, and I had to remind him of my views on being with someone who was still in a relationship. He respected this, and we didn't start officially dating until he had ended his prior relationship. In hindsight, I see that he jumped from one woman to the other, and I'm sure many people got hurt in the process. I also have my doubts about how honest Casper was, but there's no point in looking back. It won't change anything and, besides, I was so in love that I had completely lost my connection to planet Earth.

We fell head over heels for one another and quickly started working together at the shop. He had a day job selling flowers wholesale, but when he finished, he would come down and help me with the closing shifts. He mainly helped with the more physical tasks, such as changing the flowers, rearranging the buckets, sweeping the storefront, etc. I remember feeling that I was being looked after, and I truly enjoyed having someone want to help me.

Casper had all the signs of someone who had been truck driving and working abroad for a long time. He had established himself in England to get away from his complicated family life, which was in pieces. We didn't see his family very often, and they only visited a few times. He would always say that his family was a picture of all the things he didn't want for his own family.

He had divorced parents who hadn't spoken to one another for twenty years. They both lived in Den Haag, where Casper had been born. His father had left his mother, and his big sister and little brother, for another woman when they were quite young. The specifics of how it had all happened were a mystery to me, but there were a lot of bad dynamics in his family. Casper always said he spoke to his dad against his mum's wishes because he needed him in his life, regardless of what he might have done to his mum. His little brother declined to have any contact with their father, but the big sister had a family life, with a husband and kids, and seemed by far the most stable of the three. I met his mother, and his sister and brother, on a trip to Holland. The mother's English wasn't great, but his brother, a truck driver, spoke it fluently. His sister had four kids and seemed to have established her own family, which came with some detachment from their mum and dad. We also visited his dad and his new wife. She was very loud, and it was clear that the past wasn't something you spoke about in this family.

As things progressed, it became apparent that we had done the right thing: we'd waited to get to know each other better, and he took the time to sever ties with his ex-girlfriend, who still kept ringing on late nights. Maybe this should have set off alarm bells. He had a studio flat, in Kingston, for a short while, but after six months of dating, we agreed to move in together. It was all done sensibly and by the book – or that's what I thought, anyway. The flat in Ealing, with the old gas heaters that seemed to mildly suffocate us, became our place. It was like a seventies movie; we were following our dreams. We were inseparable but also poor, and I had bought the oldest white van I could buy for £500, in order to make deliveries for larger events. We were together as a couple, and we also worked together. I did have a few doubts, and noticed him spending money on things we didn't need, but he put it down to being spontaneous, and I went along with it. Quickly, the shop began to seem like his, as well. He decided to stop working for the wholesaler I'd met him through. The shop was getting more and more popular, and we were doing well enough to pay him a salary.

We soon moved into a flat on Richmond Hill, to be closer to the shop. It was a really beautiful old place – no double glazing, and the smallest kitchen in the world, but we were excited. It was on the first floor, up some squeaky stairs, and with the toilet behind the kitchen. The living room was bright and looked out on a shared garden. It was our first real nest, and we had visions of growing old together and having kids. All the doubts that had been creeping up on me for the past six months were washed away in an instant.

Casper was now helping on an everyday basis, and because I felt he was the one, I made him a director (with no shares, though, as he hadn't put any money into the shop). We believed that we were creating a huge business, with the potential to expand into many more shops. I gave him all the rights to deal with bank accounts, accountants, suppliers, markets, and every-thing else. At that point, it didn't matter – I was besotted. I'd worked really hard to save up the money to start my business, and this was a huge thing for me to share with him, but I felt that our love would never end. He worked so hard in the shop that the doubts faded away as quickly as they crept in.

We had loads of fun and crazy times together. My friends loved him, and they were all good judges of character. Some of my girlfriends even fancied him – it was that good. The old group of friends, including Daniel and Camilla, thought he was sound.

Camilla, who I was close to, had married Steve, a mutual friend, and they'd bought a flat together. She thought Casper was caring and was always helpful when friends needed a lift or some help moving. If anyone had a problem, Casper would be the first to offer to help. The customers loved him, and we came to be known in Richmond as the happy, sociable couple who ran the flower shop. From the outside, everything must have looked perfect – and it was.

Business got better, and Polly started working for me (or 'us', I should say) a few days a week. But even as business improved, I started noticing parking fines on a regular basis. I often turned to him and said, "Babe, can't you just remember to move the van?"

His answer would be, "They shouldn't have fined me anyway, because the sign's missing a few letters – you can't even read it properly, it's not legal," or, "It's crazy you can't park there – everyone does it anyway."

I should have picked up on his inability to take responsibility for his mistakes. Again, my only excuse is that I was so in love.

The honeymoon period began to fade, and I started noticing more parking tickets, his high mobile bills, and the cash withdrawals on nights he was at the pub with his mates. Some of his 'company expenditures' were a bit of a stretch.

When I confronted him, he would say, "Hun, would I have spent this money if I didn't believe in us?" or, "Babe, trust me, I know it's a good deal, and if it doesn't work out, I'll take a job as a bus driver to make the money back," or, "I had to lend Jake some money for his mortgage; he got sacked again." He convinced me every time. What bothered me was the fact that it was my money he used every time he had a great idea or had to help out a friend. I rationalised it with different excuses. *My friends couldn't be that wrong*, I'd think, and, *He's so kind and genuine, and he works hard.* Facts stand no chance, when you're in love.

We started living the high life, socialising with clients and joining them for prosecco in the gardens of their huge mansions. We were going to the personal events of fashion people and rock stars on the hill, after creating the floral decorations for their dinner parties and weddings, and hitting the night life hard – we lived in the fast lane. Often, the nights were finished with passion, and we weren't careful with protection; we were in love and careless. A year after we moved in together, I became pregnant. I'd felt strange for a few weeks and, before my period was even due, I took a pregnancy test. At first, it was blank. I sighed with relief, wiped myself, flushed, and picked up the test. Then, I checked one more time to be sure, and there they were: two red stripes, clear as the colours of the Danish flag. Red and white, Danish dynamite. My heart dropped, and I screamed silently. I went into the living room and found Casper sitting on the couch with a can of beer. He looked at me and his face fell. He knew I was going to tell him something important. I think, in his mind, he was probably going through all the things I could have caught him doing.

"I'm pregnant," I said. His jaw dropped.

"How did that happen?"

I couldn't believe it – maybe it was the shock that had invited an outburst like that. I looked at him, and he was trembling. One eye began blinking; it was almost as if a vein was pumping his eye out. My legs were wobbly and soft, and I felt slightly nauseous. I sent him out to get some more beers, cigarettes, and a Chinese takeaway. I needed a minute for myself, and I also needed what was to become my last beer and cigarette for a long time, if this test was accurate. Casper grabbed me, kissed me passionately, took the van keys, and ran out of the door. I sat on the couch and put my face in my hands, trying to breathe calmly. After the initial, mind-numbing shock, I decided that this was going to be celebrated. I put my hand on my belly and suddenly felt that I was the happiest woman alive. I trembled and felt the urge to protect. All the problems, issues, and doubts faded away in the excitement of having a baby with the man I loved. I picked up the phone and dialled my mum and dad's number. My father had always been eager to have a grandchild, and now I could tell him he was going to have one.

Casper came back after two hours, drunk. I wasn't amused, but I'd been talking to my parents for most of his absence. It turned out Casper had gone to the pub and told everyone, buying them rounds, and I couldn't help thinking that it had come out of my account while he'd gotten to play the big man. He was insecure and had this need to have a big car and live in a big house in the right area. He felt that his materialism gave people the idea that he was a businessman, when the reality was that we were simply hard-working people and had a normal life, just like everyone else.

My parents, who were over the moon, had cried over the phone. I told Casper and he hardly responded. We ate the Chinese and I had one beer. He got even more drunk, contrary to my expectation that he would sober up after the food, and smoked all the cigarettes – I had a toke or two, but it's incredible how quickly you begin to feel guilty about your unborn child.

The same evening, while I was cleaning up the Chinese and getting slowly irritated about his behaviour, he phoned his family to tell them the news. I remember very clearly his sister asking, "With who?" I was immediately offended but, looking back, I see she knew him better than I did.

I went to bed happy, dizzy, and deflated about Casper and the pregnancy. I told myself it was the shock of it all, and that he would be in a better place the next day. I could hear him snore from the couch in the living room, the telly still playing some sports game.

The next day, we rolled into our new honeymoon period, and Casper started changing his ways. He stopped going to the pubs as much, and the parking tickets stopped arriving – he seemed to be growing up, day by day. It was a good job, because we needed to change our ways, with this baby coming.

I remember our first scan. I was about three months pregnant, by then. We were very nervous, as I'd been sick too often and had lost weight. I simply threw up at anything: the smell of paper, the smell of people, the smell of aftershave – I was terribly ill, to the point where I had to take medicine every day. My gums bled every time I brushed my teeth, and when I tasted blood, I would throw up again – I'd collapse on the bathroom floor and just lie there for a while. It was the first time I appreciated the whole 'carpets on the bathroom floor' thing, as it meant I could lie there without being cold and, after a while, it felt quite comfortable.

Because of the hormones and the nausea, I was in tears all the time. Going to the shop every day became a chore, as I suddenly had the urge to retch whenever I smelled the raffia I used to tie my flowers. Clients tried to help daily with advice, and someone told me to eat ginger biscuits and drink ginger beer. I ate and drank them constantly, and haven't touched them since. One client was so sweet, coming in with Chinese acupuncture wrist bands that helped with my morning sickness. The shop was a huge part of the local community, and it felt good to be so looked after, even by people who were just clients.

We arrived at Kingston hospital and sat in the waiting room. The radiologist came to collect us and asked me to lie down on a bench, which had been made ready with a long piece of paper towel. I was so scared that something was wrong, or that all the vomiting had damaged the baby somehow. The radiologist circled the probe in a gel pool on my belly and, suddenly, she was smiling. She told me there was a good reason for the sickness: I had double the hormones. I had no idea what she meant. She turned the monitor around, and there were two white balls on the screen.

"You're expecting twins," she said, smiling. Casper was so

happy he started laughing. I turned around and slapped him, jumped off the bed, and ran out of the room. I sat on the first hospital toilet I could find, locked myself in, and just sobbed. Twins? My imagination had told me that I could handle a baby under the arm – I'd chat to clients and stroll through the shop doors with a pram. Now, there was no way I'd be able to fit a twin pram through the shop doors, and I'd have no hands free to arrange flowers. Worse still, my tits would never be the same again, and I wondered if, and how, they were both going to come out of me, and what my lower region would end up like. Eventually, the nurse came to get me, and I went home. On the way, I sat in the van, crying and trying to digest what the radiologist had just said. Casper tried to calm me down, but something in me was terrified. I couldn't comprehend what had just been said. Arriving at the flat, I curled up on the couch. I was supposed to call my mum and tell her how it had gone, but instead I cried for hours and didn't show up to the shop. Polly was working at the time, and Casper went down to tell her that I would call her later. My mum phoned, and I couldn't speak at all, I was sobbing so much.

She kept saying, "Whatever it is, we'll deal with it."

I could tell she was getting more and more worried, and I finally got the words out.

"I'm expecting twins, Mum," I said, and she gave a joyful scream. "We'll get through it together," she said. "Don't worry about anything – we'll help you."

She undertook the task of calling everyone, as I was exhausted. She phoned my father, who was in an important meeting with the Danish forensics team, and had told his secretary that he was not to be disturbed.

He picked up the phone and said, "It better be important!"

Mum replied, "Your daughter is expecting twins! Chew on that!" and hung up the phone.

My father cut the meeting short and went home crying. According to my mum, he's barely stopped since. He had always wanted to be a grandfather. Once, he tried to bribe one of my friends into convincing me to get knocked up, as he was losing faith in me ever getting serious with anyone. She actually accepted his challenge and spent several weeks trying to convince me that children would be beneficial to everyone.

The Crazy Kitchen

Being pregnant with twins was challenging. I had to consciously try not to fart when I bent down to grab flowers for a client, along with avoiding making gagging noises when I smelled their aftershave. I craved McDonald's cheeseburgers and cream cakes, and if I didn't get a cream cake when I wanted it, I could simply cry – it felt like a matter of life or death. The cravings were very powerful, and I never realised when they were coming. Camilla was pregnant too, and her cravings were citrus fruits and apples – I mean, some things are just ridiculously unfair.

Appointments with the midwife became more frequent, now that they knew I was having twins. I was signed on to an antenatal class, and I showed up to the first session only to discover that I was the only one expecting twins. When we held our baby dolls and learned how to breastfeed, and how important breastmilk is for newborn children, I raised my hand to ask how to cope with two babies. The midwife gave me an extra doll and told me to assume the 'rugby position'. Everyone laughed and I smiled politely. Later on, I sobbed my eyes out on the toilet.

Your dignity goes when you're pregnant; there's no other way to explain it. I can't remember how many doctors' hands I've had up my vagina. My boy was the baby expected to come out first, as he was lying on my bladder. My baby girl, on the other hand, had her feet down and was resting her head up. She was using my ribs as a climbing frame. During another of the antenatal classes, we were shown, in graphic detail, how twins in different positions are born. In my case, the midwife would basically insert her whole hand inside of me, up to the wrist, and drag the second baby out by her feet. It made me dread that I'd never be the same again, from the belly button and down.

Don't get me wrong; my first and foremost concern was for the babies. I was very aware of the high risk that comes with twin pregnancies and was super grateful for having healthy, kicking foetuses. I was, like most expectant mums, very happy and smothered in Clarins oil to avoid stretch marks, as well as Anusol cream to fight haemorrhoids. I was downing Gaviscon as if it was about to sell out, as my heartburn was killing me, and I went everywhere with a Tena pad, just in case I sneezed or giggled and wet my pants. Despite all this, I was very grateful.

During one midwife visit, I asked when the three months' tiredness would end, as I was about five months pregnant. She told me that with twins, the fatigue doesn't end, as your body produces double the hormones and spends double the energy on feeding the babies. With constant nausea to top it all off, I was already exhausted. Needless to say, I was no yummy mummy. There were no great hair days, no smart clothes, none of the stuff that typically comes with being an expectant mum in an area like Richmond.

Considering how infrequently Casper and I had partied together prior to my pregnancy, stopping drinking and smoking wasn't hard for me. What I found more difficult was people around me getting pissed and half-shouting the same things over and over again. I'd have to wipe their saliva off my face and comfort them as they often broke down and cried about some emotional turmoil brought to the surface. Of course, I didn't give a toss – I was heavily pregnant! All I could think of was food and when the night buffet would be coming out. It's only when you become pregnant that these things start to annoy you; when your kids are actually born, you can't wait to get back out there to spray saliva on people's faces and yell about how great it is to be a mum and how calm and brilliant your kids are, even when they're not.

During the pregnancy, my relationship with Casper started to crumble quickly. He tried to start a business with someone else in the flower industry as a wholesaler and failed miserably, but of course, he claimed it wasn't his fault. Same song, different record. My business was going well and, by this point, I had three girls working for me. However, we started facing heavier financial difficulties due to Casper's attempts to start his own business. My parents often bailed us out when they could, but I started to realise that my kids' father was irresponsible with money. It was putting a huge strain on us. Casper himself was in total denial – he never seemed to understand that his choices were his responsibility. It was always someone else's fault.

One day, I came home and found a letter from the council. Thinking it was about the business, I opened it. As I read it, I started to lose my mind; he owed thousands in parking fines, which he'd hidden from me. I wondered when enough would be enough. Had my family unit already broken down before it'd had a chance to start? Was I giving up too easily? I had hormones messing with my head, and when he got home that day, I just screamed at him. He had lied, put us in debt, and wasn't admitting anything. The phone bills had increased, he'd taken money out of the business account before making sure bills were paid, and we were behind on our rent. This was despite the fact that the business was doing very well. He simply lived above his means and was becoming even more reckless with money.

That night, many tears were shed, but in the end, I asked him to pack his stuff. I told him that I would go for a walk and, by the time I was back, I wanted him gone. It was one month before the twins were due, but the letter from the council was the drop that made the cup spill over. I walked out after our argument and sat on a bench on Richmond Hill, freezing my butt off in the November air and talking to Polly on the phone. She tried to calm me down and was shocked to hear what he had done. I was sobbing – I felt ashamed and couldn't bring myself to call my parents. Between all the money they'd lent us and the fact that they were on their way to come and support us, I just felt so embarrassed. Things had seemed to go downhill so fast, and I was unable to figure out how I'd missed the signs. It dawned on me that they'd always been there, but I wasn't ready to admit that I'd have to be a fool to stay with him. I was carrying his babies and tried to figure out where the Casper I had met in the beginning had gone. This was meant to be a stress-free time in my life – Casper was supposed to be taking care of me. I felt I was adding two kids to the kid I already had at home.

He had followed me, and eventually found me, after trying to get hold of me for hours. My butt was really cold by this point. He apologised and said he would straighten up and would pay the tickets off himself. He'd started working for a delivery company, but at his wage, it would have taken a year to pay the bills off, so we were still in money trouble. Still, I reluctantly went back to him. I couldn't face being on my own. The thought of being a single mum was scarier than being with a total fuck-up, so I comforted myself by hoping that he would straighten himself out.

My parents arrived about two weeks before my due date. They rented a studio flat for six months so that they could be on hand to help us. I was so grateful. They lived on Onslow Road, which sat between Marlborough Road (where we lived) and the shop, which was on Eton Street. Their visit also made it easier for Casper to make money – he could work while I manned the shop with the help of my father, and my mother helped with the cooking and cleaning. I enjoyed the fact that we weren't working together as much. It felt like a break from all the troubles. The twins were growing steadily stronger. I had, with Casper, decided to call our son 'Magnus' and our daughter 'Pepper'.

The kids were due in mid-December, 2005. I could still carry on running the shop, but it would take me about an hour to walk up Richmond Hill from the shop to our flat. I had Braxton Hicks constantly, but worked up until my last visit to the midwife, which was one week before I gave birth. There, the midwife confirmed I was one centimetre dilated. Magnus's head was down and ready for kick-off. There had been several false alarms and, finally, the midwife decided to induce me at thirty-eight weeks pregnant.

I went to hospital and was ushered into a ward with six other women, all of whom were lying on beds. We were lying so close to each other that I couldn't help but bond a little with the mum next to me. She was drinking tea and shared her biscuits with me. In Denmark, we'd have been eating liquorice or open sandwiches and drinking coffee, but it was the same ritual, really. The doctor came in to speak to me and pulled the curtain over so I could pretend the person lying next to me didn't know what was going on. Putting her rubber gloves on and squeezing a bit of lube over her fingers, she had a feel around in my lower parts to make sure things were running smoothly. It never stopped being awkward. Afterwards, the curtain was pulled back and I returned to my tea, biscuits, and chatting, with nothing more than a redder face to show for it.

I spent three days in that ward. The women came and went around me, and by the time I was finally called in, the whole set of women had turned over. After eight visits from different doctors (all of them shuffling their hands up my private parts), it became too much, and I told the last doctor that if he got near my fanny and told me I was still only one centimetre dilated, he would have his hand chopped off. Sadly, my threats didn't work, and after seventy-two hours in labour, they decided I should have a C-section. My son's heart rate was a bit quicker than they were happy with, something they attributed to stress. They took me to the Caesarean ward and, suddenly, I had my own room, my own bed, and my own nurse – it was heaven.

I was taken into a surgery room and weighed myself, which was quite a bummer, considering that I had, for months, hidden the scales at home, but at that point, you just want your babies to come out healthy. I was placed on a bed and given an epidural. I lay down and, when I looked up, my foot was there, right on top of my face. It turned out they were inserting the urine catheter. Looking around, I realised there were eight people in the room: nurses, paediatricians, midwives, doctors, and others. I was suddenly delirious, and my pain faded as the drugs kicked in, so I started singing and shouting about how sorry I was not to have had the chance to have a Brazilian wax, or to have at least trimmed the beast, and this would be the last time I got knocked up on a drunken night – I think I went on for a while, which, needless to say, I felt quite embarrassed about afterwards. Casper was there for the whole surgery and, despite our troubles, we were again swept away by the feeling that we were part of something unique. He wasn't there for many of the days I was in hospital, as he was busy building his second business. The truth was, I was happier at the hospital without him.

As most mums will tell you, my world crumbled as soon as the babies came out, and a new world began. The first cry was Magnus. He was born at 15:54 p.m. on the 19th of December, 2005. He was laid on my chest, where I held him close to my face so that I could kiss him. He looked at me with his beautiful, brown eyes. He was 34cm long, had lots of black hair, and weighed only 2.7 kilos. He just looked at me and stopped crying as soon as I spoke to him. I fell in love instantly. Then, it was Pepper's turn, but she was clinging to my ribs, and they really had to give her a heave before she came out all blue. It felt longer, but she was born at 15:55 p.m., exactly one minute later, and weighed 2.5 kilos and was 37cm long. I couldn't hold her instantly, as she hadn't taken a breath yet. They took her aside and I could sense some commotion. It took her a while to scream, but after lots of back-rubbing, she did. Those seconds of lying there and waiting for a sound felt like eternity. I was absolutely broken – I felt a huge love, unlike anything I'd ever felt before. Nothing can prepare you for that love but, at the same time, you also give birth to fear. Feeling this kind of love created in me, along with the fear of losing it, was earth-shattering. I began to feel the lioness I would have to become stirring inside of me. The lioness has pulled me through every single test and trial I've had to survive since giving birth to these beautiful twins. They are my cubs, and it's my job to protect them.

Magnus and Pepper were tiny babies, but they were healthy and only a little jaundiced. My afterbirth experience, however, wasn't great. My parents had arranged a private room at the hospital, which was awesome, but the care was hindered by the fact that it was during the holidays and only days before Christmas. The room had a large bed, with a window to the back alleys of a chain of houses, and it had its own bathroom, with a bath. It was a luxury to have the room.

A day had gone by, and all I'd done was constantly look at the two most amazing creatures I'd ever seen. I hadn't had any visitors yet, apart from my parents and Casper's mum. Magnus and Pepper shared a hospital cot, and they slept a lot. I'd tried to breastfeed Magnus, but he'd had problems latching on, and a shortage of midwives, due to the season, made it almost impossible for me to get help. I had to start on milk supplements, feeding Magnus from a baby bottle for premature babies, due to his size, with Pepper under the other arm, feeding from me. I hardly slept, and Casper, who had slept on the floor of the room for the first night, didn't help much. He didn't wake up when Magnus and Pepper cried, and I had to shout him conscious, since I couldn't move very quickly. Afterwards, the tiredness was replaced by the euphoria of my babies making me able to smile all the way through it. After twenty-four hours, I was told by the nurses to go take a shower to help soak up the plaster over my C-section, so they could help peel away the dressing and stitches. Sat in the shower, I was forgotten, and I had the bright idea to take off my own bandages, which resulted in me passing out from the look of the line where the cut had been made. They found me about ten minutes later, crying and shaking, the whole time feeling stupid, as I was lying there naked. They were apologising for the error and tucked me back into bed, talking about what a beautiful job the surgeon had done. Later on that same day, Casper said he had to go home to sleep for the night as he was knackered. His mother, who had arrived to meet her grandchildren earlier that day, agreed that her son needed rest. I had to stop myself from shouting about what I'd just been through.

Here I was, lying in the hospital bed after seventy-two hours in labour, having just passed out in the shower, with no partner and two tiny babies to feed. I'm sure now that this was a sign of things to come, but again, I was too preoccupied by my two amazing babies to give it much thought. The midwives and nurses looking after me were all big, strong, beautiful Jamaican women who hadn't been impressed when I'd asked to book a private room. The thought of going back to a room with six other women and sharing biscuits wasn't something I could cope with – my tits were sore as hell, and I'd just been cut open. Nevertheless, I had my room, and after my ordeal, I slept while the kids were treated for jaundice. They were lying under a lamp right next to me, with nurses checking in on us every thirty minutes. Each time, I woke up when a nurse came in and looked at her as a lioness would at someone touching her cubs. When the nurse left, I'd gaze from my bed over at their small feet and hands moving slightly, and I would fall asleep with a smile on my face until the next nurse came in. The stay in hospital was my time to connect with my kids. They were so quiet and smelled so good. I remember feeling that everything had been worth it.

I was allowed to go home after three days. Coming home with kids was great, but also challenging. We still had Casper's mother staying with us, who deemed it fit to tell me, on my first night home, that I shouldn't forget to love their father more than the kids. I was shocked and told her that wasn't possible. I said it was a weird thing to bring up, and the two loves were completely different. We quickly decided to agree to disagree. The lioness in me was already starting to show, and I shut her down in less than ten minutes, which was certainly unusual. I had learned to say 'no'! I was beginning to make the transition from being a people-pleaser to sticking to my guns about what felt right. Becoming a mum was a strength for me. Nevertheless, she kept on insisting that everything I did was wrong, which kept me on my toes. Consequently, we didn't get along at all, and she left a few days later, on poor terms. She had crossed my boundaries, criticising rather than helping. She had commented on every detail of baby bath, baby feed, supplement milks, and it was never-ending in terms of what I could do better. By the time she left, the kids were a week old. My parents had stayed in the background to give Casper some time with his family.

As a surprise, my sister Taina came to meet her niece and nephew. She was the best auntie and, very quickly, my world seemed fairly normal around me. I felt more balanced with all my family there, even if it was just for a short while. The shop was showered with gifts from clients to congratulate us. It was heart-warming and showed we had a place in many people's hearts. We couldn't walk down the road, or even just to my parents in Richmond Park, without being met with smiling recognition and congratulations.

Both kids had stomach problems, which is apparently common in newborn twins, and as a result, I barely slept for several weeks. As I had read a lot and taken classes, I was as prepared as I could be, but Casper was useless; he couldn't handle the lack of sleep, and our relationship quickly started turning bad (or 'worse', you could say). We stopped communicating, and I was left to look after the kids. The thing was, I was happy with this turn of events – if he wasn't interested in them, I didn't want him nearby.

I would wake up some nights and roll to one side and feed one child, and then the next baby would wake up, and I would roll over and feed with the other breast. This was how they lost their shape! I laid down on my back and used my elbows to find my nipples. It was surreal; I'd never realised how much of her body a woman gives to create life.

The children were beautiful. I could just sit and look at them, kiss them, touch them, and keep smelling them – I loved smelling them. I still do, but now I'm greeted with a "Muuuum! Stop it, it's weird!" Things change so quickly.

I was left to do everything and, despite the midwife's advice, I had to go back to work after only three weeks of maternity leave. The business was struggling, and Casper's family weren't able to help, either financially or practically. It was all left to my parents to assist. I remember, on the first day, leaving the twins with my parents and walking down to the shop – it was so strange. It was odd not having my babies next to me – it felt wrong and empty – but if I wanted to survive the financial crisis, I had to go back to work. Every day in the shop, I would have comments from clients as to why on Earth I wasn't home with my babies. I couldn't have agreed more, but it was like they had kicked me in my belly while I was lying down. When I tried to explain that the business was struggling, many women only shook their heads and had a look on their faces that said there must be another way – there wasn't much understanding. Trying to get the pram through the door confirmed one of my anticipations, and I had to knock a wall down in the back so I could access the shop on the days I had the twins but still needed to work. Casper lost his driving job (it was, of course, 'not his fault'), and he was still trying to get his new business together. It was a flower stall with another guy, who would be the investor. I had given up on our relationship by this point – we were simply coexisting. I didn't tell my parents, as it was embarrassing and humiliating. I had no faith in this project, and I completely ignored his lack of interest in our lives.

My parents helped so much, in those first few months. They cooked and cleaned and loved the babies as if they were their own. They were truly respectful to me and Casper and, to give us our own space, they helped us financially as much as they could afford. However, I was already feeling the distance; I simply had no respect for Casper as a father. He ignored the kids, and the sleepless nights were too much for him. One night, he even got up, picked up our crying son, and screamed his head off about how tired he was of it. Magnus and Pepper were, at that point, only three months old. From that night forward, I took all the night shifts. Months went by, and he did less and less. He was hotheaded and wasted his days down at the pub with friends of his that I didn't even know. Sometimes, I couldn't get hold of him at all, and he'd come home the next morning. I know that my parents saw all of it happen, but they never got involved. They knew that having twins while trying to maintain a struggling business would take a toll on any couple, but they did wonder why I did as much as I did. Looking back, maybe I loved the control – after all, if I did everything, it would be done my way. If I did everything, I wouldn't have to expect anything from him and, ultimately, we would argue less. Having no expectations kept me from being disappointed. Nonetheless, I was in total survival mode, and remained so for years after.

My parents had to leave after six months, and we decided to hire a part-time nanny – an amazing Brazilian lady named

Isabelle. When she'd worked with us for a month, she told me she was expecting, so I knew we only had her for seven more months. I was happy for her, but again, I felt like I couldn't breathe because of all the obstacles that kept coming at me. As soon as I conquered one, the next would show up. Isabelle and I fell into a daily routine while Casper made deliveries, closed the shop, and sometimes went to the market. We had to let two girls go and soon, only Polly was helping on a part-time basis. As the months went by, my relationship with Casper didn't improve, and his stupid behaviour was still racking up the bills.

I suffered from bad mastitis, a severe breast infection, and had to be admitted to hospital, as my temperature had risen to forty-one degrees. Mastitis is a kind of infection where the milk gets congested and builds up in the breasts as hard cysts. It turned out that I had five cysts in one breast and three in another. The milk was slowly poisoning my body, and I was admitted to Kingston hospital late one afternoon. Two nurses came into my room to get me ready for the examination. Casper was outside, looking after the kids in the waiting room, getting irritated that he couldn't get on with his day. The hospital smell was making me feel even worse. The nurses told me to relax and the specialist, Dr. Nilson, came in. He was a very short man, almost bald, and was quite round in his build.

He hardly looked at me as he said, "So, what do we have here?"

He examined me and stuck a long needle through the skin, right next to my nipple. He tweaked it around until he found a cyst he could drain. I nearly bit the nurse's hand, and I was crying so loudly that one nurse began to stroke my face and spoke to me like I was a child. The liquid that Dr. Nilson removed was cappuccino-coloured – it was breast milk that had literally gone off. When he'd finished, he told me to come back the next day for the same procedure, as I needed to have all the cysts drained. My whole body was shaking, and I had sweat pearls running down my temples. I asked if I could have painkillers or a local anaesthetic during these procedures, as it was more painful than labour had been, and like a typical male doctor, he said there was no need, as it would be done quickly. I wondered if he'd say the same if I carried out the same procedure on his balls. I shook my head – I felt sick and exhausted, almost delirious.

I scraped myself off the bench and walked slowly to the waiting room, where Casper was chatting up the nurses, looking less irritated than when I'd left him. He stood by the desk and leaned up against the corner. He was smiling and very flirty, telling them how hard it was to be the parent of newborn twins, while he rocked the twins' car seat with one foot. The nurses were flattered that this handsome, seemingly very hands-on father would give them some attention, and it hit me that my life was like a comedy. If only they knew what he was really like! I asked to go home and got on with the day, whereas Casper left again as soon as we got back. He said I looked perkier and must have felt that it was okay to leave me alone. I put the kids next to me in our bed and fell asleep with them.

When the children were nine months old, I was writing letters, pleading for payment plans for the parking tickets Casper had accrued. We had also fallen behind on our rent again, and I had to write letters to our landlord, begging him not to throw us out. Then I received a £600 mobile bill. Casper swore to me that it had nothing to do with him, so I contacted the mobile company, who told me that they would investigate. They phoned me back, and all they could tell me was that the numbers would have to have been dialled in order to be registered. One morning, soon after, Casper couldn't find his phone – he was already late to his part-time driving job and, eventually, he had to leave without it. It was me who had hidden his phone. When he left, I pulled the phone out and started investigating. His phone was full of images of naked and half-naked women. His texts were raunchy, too – he'd been texting women for sex. I contacted my accountant and asked him to investigate all our bank statements. I found gambling arrears on our bank statements – they were taken a little at a time, so they wouldn't be discovered. My blood was boiling. I just kept swearing at him in my mind, and sometimes out loud. Of course, I had to continue to work and smile at customers, even though all I wanted to do was explain that I wasn't suffering from slapped cheek syndrome, but was instead with an arsehole. I also had to pay the mobile company, as it was on the same account as my work phone, and I couldn't afford for it to be switched off.

When Casper got home, I confronted him. He denied gambling and said it was fraud, and I actually believed him when he swore on his kids' lives. The bank refunded the amounts, which had come out over three months. His excuse for the sex-texting was that he felt I loved the kids more than him. I said I did. He said he wanted to be loved and touched – we hadn't had any fun, he said, since the twins had arrived. I tried to compose myself and said to him that if he wanted to turn me on, he should do the dishes now and again, clean the flat, cook some dinner, bathe the kids, you name it – at the very least, he should try not to get us into financial trouble! Then I would spread my legs and maybe even get something out of it myself! Who was this man? We argued for weeks afterwards, and I was too embarrassed to tell any of my friends, apart from Polly, who just laughed and said maybe he should try to hump the computer and see how sexy that was. She said that everyone knew it wasn't real women behind the numbers Casper had been calling. It was all computer-generated, and as for the online messages, it could have been an old man replying to him from behind a computer screen and sending photos of sexy women. It was idiots like my partner they were cashing in on.

Casper kept apologising over the following weeks, and he eventually convinced me that it was the transition from a two- to a four-person family that had made him lose it a bit. Looking back, I think that if he'd had the opportunity to move somewhere else or meet someone else, he would have left. We were stuck together because of the financial issues, and because of my ongoing fear of doing it on my own. I hadn't realised that I was already done with him.

Love on Bruschetta and Furry Balls

The fear of caring for two children on my own was still worse than the thought of staying with Casper. It was the uncertainty – if I left him, I didn't know what would happen, both with the kids and with my financial situation. At least I knew what was in front of me with Casper: unhappiness. Additionally, it seemed too early to give up on my family unit. Casper stayed because he had nowhere else to go, no money, and no real job – just absolutely nothing. He spent more than what he earned in the shop, and the debt was still piling up.

When the kids were ten months old, a client asked me whether I was interested in buying their house, as they were relocating. They knew we were renting and that we might want to start investing. I went to see the house and fell in love with it. It was a red-brick house on the corner of a cul-de-sac, with its own driveway and small front and back gardens. The client's wife was an artist, and she had bought many flowers from me. There were yellow daffodils everywhere in the gardens and roses of all different colours. The house was a stone's throw from the river and a ten-minute bike ride from the town centre. Inside the house, things became even more idyllic. It had two full bedrooms and a small bedroom or storage room, a bathroom, a living room, and garden doors to the small garden. The kitchen was small, but again, it felt perfect. My parents, who had by now been back living in Denmark for four months, helped me apply for a mortgage with a financial advisor based in London. It made sense, as the mortgage was less than paying rent for our flat. As Casper had no money whatsoever, and only bad debts that we were both still paying off, I decided to buy the house under just my name. The financial advisor mentioned that Casper wouldn't pass a credit check and could jeopardise the application, so it made sense to leave him off it. Luckily, my parents were able to give me a sum of money as an advance inheritance to put down as a deposit. They rearranged some of their own finances to be able to help me.

It felt like being the old me again – independent, strong, and a loner. Even my parents advised me against including Casper, which was the first and only time they'd ever gotten involved in our relationship. As my father pointed out, Casper technically owed him a lot of money for always helping us get out of trouble, and Casper hadn't even acknowledged this.

Papers were signed, mortgages went through, and we moved into the house in January, 2006. It actually felt like a fresh start. I felt that if we could do this and get through all the crap, maybe we had a chance. We were definitely getting better; the house gave us a purpose, and the shop started making some money again. It was a slow process, but as we were still paying off Casper's debts, we didn't have much to play with. In addition to his parking debts, we were also paying off the loans he'd taken out to set up his own company. Still, it felt like there was a light at the end of the tunnel. The move made it feel as if we were physically moving away from our problems, and I learned to ignore them. I wanted to be positive and open, not to battle all the time.

The move was exhausting, and it was scary to have a mortgage. I was afraid that I wouldn't be able to pay it every month, but it worked out to be cheaper than our rented flat, and I suppose I knew, deep down, that I could sell the house, if the shit hit the fan. We also decided to put Casper through a gardening course. He was the instigator, but it seemed to make sense; we'd be able to sell high-quality gardening services through the shop, once he finished the course. I paid £1000 in college fees, and he was really keen to get started. It was nice to see a little of the old Casper I'd fallen in love with, but he was still only a shadow of the man I'd once known. I still wasn't able to find the love for him I'd once had. I wasn't attracted to him, and our sex life had completely dried up. I simply had no respect for him. I suggested couples therapy, but he refused. He thought it was the financial problems he'd caused that had brought this on, and that he could fix it by showing me he could change.

I had two beautiful children, a running business, and had just bought a house. The relationship was what it was, but it was far less important than the other things in my life. I had been exhausted by his mischief, and I came to accept that this was our normal relationship: him making a mess, and me sweeping it up behind him. Payment agreements came with him, as a package. Lucky me.

When the kids were about fourteen months old, our sweet Isabelle had to leave us. I decided to try an au pair, as they were typically cheaper, and we needed someone to look after our kids. It seemed strange to me that childcare in England was so lacking; in Denmark, you could place your children in full-time care for about £300 a month, as the government wanted you back at work. Here, the cheapest nursery we could find was £1400 a month. It was twice my mortgage, so an au pair was an easy decision, financially. We were advised to look on Gumtree, a website which was very popular, at that time.

The first woman we accepted seemed nice. She was from the Czech Republic – her name was Rene, and although she hadn't been abroad before, she had experience looking after kids. When Rene arrived, she looked so young and sweet. She had a tiny figure and short hair, and her clothing seemed very dated, reminiscent of the '90s. She looked much younger than her age of eighteen, and her English was definitely better in writing to the point that I wondered whether she'd had someone help her interact with us over email. She told us she had a sister living in Acton, so we knew she would be away for quite a lot of weekends, which was a win for us and her. When she'd been with us for a week, it became pretty clear that she didn't have much experience. I had to take a step back and explain everything to her carefully. I trusted her, but it definitely wasn't going to be smooth sailing.

One day, I came home slightly earlier than normal, and she was so glued to MTV that she didn't notice me come in. The kids were on her lap watching MTV too, which was showing young singers with their tits on display. I had to give her a warning. I'm sure the kids didn't realise what they were watching and, to be honest, in Denmark, you're considered a prude if you don't have your tits out on the beach, but I still thought that playing with a train or building blocks would be more appropriate.

Two weeks passed, and it was a struggle. Our third weekend was coming up, and she went to see her sister on the Friday. She was meant to come back on Sunday evening, but didn't arrive until Monday afternoon. She had been partying hard and, while I didn't blame her (she was from the countryside, so London must have seemed like a fairground), I didn't want my kids in her care while she was still drunk from the weekend. I asked her to leave the same day. I was angry and spoke to her sister, who was quite embarrassed and assured me that she would be safe with her and apologised for the inconvenience, and then I wished her well.

Back on Gumtree, I corresponded with another girl, who also happened to be Czech. Our brilliant Anezka had been a nursery teacher in the Czech Republic and was a few years older than Rene. She came over and was very charismatic. I had a good feeling about her, and she knew exactly what she was doing. She didn't know anyone in England, so she would be staying in every weekend. It was challenging. Everything was shared: the one toilet, the one bath. We'd had to move the kids from her room, and so they mainly slept with us, but at the end of the day, Anezka gave us more flexibility, and the business was really booming again, thank god, and needed my attention. Polly fell pregnant, and we were preparing for her to have six months maternity leave.

Months went by, and we helped Anezka get a bank card and start a course in business accountancy, as it was something she was interested in. After a few months, she began to make friends. The kids absolutely loved her, and she was great with them, which allowed me to work constantly while Casper carried on with his gardening course. We managed to get a few new clients during his course, which was apparently going well – he was balancing the work with his part-time job as a driver, and he was actually making some money. Unfortunately, after a few months, we got a letter from Casper's college informing us that if he didn't show up for class, they would have to throw him out of college. He told me he hadn't been going because the shop was too busy – the same old excuses. The truth was, he simply wasn't interested. He had again ignored the college's phone calls and hadn't communicated with them at all about his absences.

After nine months in the house, the problems started piling up, and I couldn't cope with having an au pair anymore. I couldn't breathe – it wasn't Anezka, it was the lack of privacy. Our house was simply too small. Thankfully, she was in the same place mentally, and we separated on good terms. I started applying for nurseries and, because I had more staff in the shop, I was able to take some time to visit them. I also found a government program that provided subsidies for having multiple children in nursery, meaning we could just about afford it. However, it did mean I had to pay more in taxes, so they still got you, in the end.

The shop had just signed a contract with BNP Paribas Real Estate and had been hired to create weekly displays for all the main offices in Victoria, so the money was really coming in. Polly became a manager and ran the shop during the day. She was getting bigger but started training a new girl to assist me when she went on maternity leave. Weddings were taking off too. Kew Gardens, BAFTA, and lots of local venues had taken us on as suppliers, and we started creating a better website and organising events, including Danish Christmas and Easter. I started throwing glogg parties to celebrate the advent which, in Denmark, starts with lighting one candle, on the first Sunday in December, in a wreath centrepiece made of pine and berries. These became a huge success and a big part of the community's winter traditions.

Anezka kept babysitting for quite a while after she left as an au pair, which helped immeasurably when I had to attend weddings and events. I helped her sign up with a nanny agency and, for a while, things went smoothly (apart from the continuing deterioration of mine and Casper's relationship). Finally, Casper's college dropped him. I had completely lost my faith in him, again.

The nursery was far enough away from our house that I had to take the car. I'd drop the kids off at eight in the morning and collect them at five, feeling guilty all the while. The extra money I earned from being able to work in the day all went to pay the £1200 nursery bill – yet again, I felt like a hamster on a wheel, but I just didn't know how to do it any differently. The housing market wasn't rising, so there was no point in selling and moving, as we'd depleted our cash reserves to pay off Casper's debts. We were coping, and the belief that my business was improving kept us going. It did keep crossing my mind that Casper had let us down with all his stupid behaviour and half-attempted business ideas, which always cost us more than they brought in. Why couldn't he grow up? I had no time to be analysing him, and he refused to talk about it.

One day, Mary, an old friend who I'd seen lots of when I'd shared a flat with Daniel in Fulham, got in touch and told me that she and John, her long-term partner, were getting married in Tuscany. All of our mutual friends were going – Camilla and Steve, Sam and Paul, the old gang from the times before we all started having children. We went without our kids – they stayed behind with my parents, who had come to visit London for a weekend. Casper became ill with a stomach bug just before we left and ended up staying in his room for most of the holiday, but my friends and I sat and drank wine in the sun and ate the most amazing food. It was a magical time. Mary and John had rented a stunning wedding venue, and everything had been paid for. On the first day, we went to visit Florence, and I had a wonderful time walking through the beautiful streets. I felt at peace for the first time in a long while, and a thought went through my mind, telling me that there were other ways of living. I still didn't speak to my friends about our problems because, when I'd tried, they'd stopped listening and had just thrown in their opinions, instead. They were all painfully aware of my financial struggles, but they didn't know how they'd accrued. That said, I felt like I'd left all my problems in London. This was sheer escapism: eating, walking, the sun on my skin, the undisturbed sleep, and no Casper. All combined, it was a balm for my soul, eating through the tar that had been building up.

Eventually, Casper made it out of his room and came with us to Florence. He wanted to pick up some medicine from a pharmacy, which I had to go in and get. I had no idea how to speak Italian, so with my arms in the air, I tried to be as graphic as possible, acting out belly movements, diarrhoea, and vomiting. After an entertaining twenty-five minute conversation, I finally got some remedies and set off to meet Casper at a restaurant on the Piazza della Signoria.

We were sitting in the restaurant, when he suddenly pulled out a box and, with his hands shaking, asked me in the most unromantic way if I wanted to marry him. I looked inside the box and found a beautiful ring with three diamonds, one for me and each of the twins.

My whole body shut down. I started talking about our problems and whether it was a good idea to consider marriage. I babbled on frantically for a while, every bone and fibre in me screaming "No way," but something in me didn't want to hurt his feelings. He looked at me and asked me if I could just say yes, so I did what so many people in relationships that aren't working do: I said, "Yes." I said yes because something inside of me wanted to try and fix our relationship; I didn't want a broken family, and I wanted to love him again. It was like a switch flipped in my brain – I put every thought and feeling into the belief that, if we got married, it would fix every problem we had. Thirty minutes earlier, I had been squatting in front of some unimpressed Italian pharmacists, and now I was engaged.

We were quiet on the drive back, and it was the oddest moment of my life. I felt my anger disappearing and fear creeping in. I was suddenly being forced to focus on 'us', and I hadn't done so for ages. I felt completely numb, and I knew it wasn't just the wine. When I saw my friend Sam at the hotel's vineyard, I asked her to come with me. We went into Sam's room and the first thing I said was, "I can't marry him." Sam looked at me. She had a very tiny frame, along with curly hair and blonde highlights. Not a hair sat wrong on her head, but her clothes looked as if she was fifty, not thirty-one.

She said, "It'll get better. Take it a day at a time; love doesn't run smoothly."

She didn't know the half of it. I hadn't told her everything, as I just couldn't handle the judgement. Sam was one of those people who was in complete control of her life – she let out all her problems on her yearly flip: she'd get hammered, cry for three hours, and then not remember anything the next day. I felt so alone, I decided to just go with the flow and see what happened, even as I felt I was making a mistake. I texted Polly about what had happened, and she replied that I could always change my mind but, for now, I should think deeper about what I really wanted my future to look like. Basically, "Don't do anything erratic until we've sat down and turned over every stone we can." 'Drink wine, and lots of it', was her last text before I switched my phone off.

Our engagement was announced that same evening, at the pre-wedding dinner, in front of sixty people. I fought back panic and started tearing up. Casper hugged me and kissed me – he loved the attention, and everyone thought I was happy, but I was struggling to breathe and just wanted to run to the airport and fly home to my babies. It was like I was on a different planet, and the whole world in front of me was moving when I couldn't. I got very drunk that night and played the happily engaged partner.

When we returned from Italy, I discovered that my parents already knew – Casper had apparently asked my father for my hand six months earlier. Why had it taken him until this trip to ask me? It kind of proved he wasn't sure about it, either, but I kept telling myself, "We can fix this." I had nothing else to go on. It seemed easier to stay than to leave.

We took a cab home from the airport. We couldn't afford it, but Casper was in a celebratory mood and wanted to forget about reality. I was too tired to protest, as I'd been drinking heavily for the preceding three days to try and forget that I was engaged.

When we arrived at the house, we found my parents waiting with champagne. We celebrated, but my chin was wobbly and I couldn't quite push my feelings down deep enough. My parents thought I was just being emotional. I hugged the kids like there was no tomorrow, and I couldn't stop smelling their hair. I didn't say anything to them; partly because they were too young to understand, and partly because it felt so wrong. I sat with the twins on the couch, looking at my unit talking away in our living room, and I wanted to scream, "Help me!" but I couldn't. I didn't even know who I'd be asking.

My parents left the next day. Somehow, I'd disconnected myself in order to survive; all I cared about were the kids and the shop, and I could tell that my parents weren't sure how I felt about the engagement. I realised that I didn't care whether they knew or not, which was a sad discovery, as I was so close to them. A lot of my secrecy was because I was ashamed of the whole situation, but I also lived by the idiotic rule that what's going on in your partnership should be between the two of you and no one else. A cry for help could have done wonders here, but after being shut down by my friends in Italy, I really thought that it was me who was at fault. I was totally lost in the abyss of relationship clichés, and I had no idea what to do. "Failure is not an option," I told myself, or, "Relationships are hard." And regarding our near-dead sex life, "Everyone has a dry spell," and, "All your friends are bored in bed with their husbands – just get a vibrator." The one thing I didn't consider was ending it.

My first night alone with Casper, I was petrified. The thought of having some sexually intense moment made my mouth (and other places) dry. I spent that first night in the kids' room, pretending I'd fallen asleep after reading them a story. I did this for several months, until it became the norm.

Their father – the man who I now call 'the most expensive sperm donor I have ever come across' – and I began struggling with each other even more, and I tried again to convince him to go to couples therapy. He again refused and instead fell back into his wild spending habits and lying about everything he did. It was his release, his means of escape – if he ignored things long enough, they'd go away. He'd gotten another delivery job, as (despite him not finishing it) we still needed to pay for his course, and he still had his debts, on top of that. The garden jobs stopped coming in – he didn't advertise it well and, even after I added it as a link on the shop's website, his business died.

I had to negotiate cheaper rates with my accountant, as the other option was letting him go. He was (and still is) irreplaceable, as I had no idea how to fill out English tax forms. I was working nearly eighty hours a week, and we still didn't have enough money. To make matters worse, Casper got the sack from his delivery job for reckless behaviour.

Every shop around us was closing down. Even established chains were closing, and everyone was panicking and holding on to their money. My private clients (many of whom were bankers) had lost their positions and could no longer afford grand floral designs. It was crazy. The wedding industry ground to a halt, and I remember seeing wedding venues and hotels offering clients free venue hire in an attempt to bring in business. In the midst of all this, one of the best things in my life happened. It was a black, brown, and white furry ball I called 'Rosie'.

Rosie was a dog I rescued. She helped me sleep well at night and was a rock for the kids. In many ways, she was my guardian angel. The first time I saw Rosie was when I went out during my lunchbreak, one day. I walked around the corner and there she was: a small, furry ball wrapped up in what looked like a towel. She was with a group of homeless people, who were harmless but drinking and shouting. I went to Anne, the lady who was carrying her, and asked what the dog's name was and if she was old enough to be away from her mum, as she was tiny. She said the puppy was twelve weeks old and her best friend. While Anne was talking, I noticed she had no teeth. Her clothes were ragged, and her hands and nails were almost black. I wondered how she could even afford to feed the dog, as she obviously couldn't afford to feed or clean herself. That's no decent life for anyone. I mentioned to her that, if she ever wanted help with the dog, or if she wanted to give it away, I had a shop up the road. I gave her directions and added that I lived in a house with a garden and had two kids who would love her lots. I just so wanted that dog with me; it was meant to be. The dog looked at me once, and the instant connection was undeniable. It was heart-breaking to walk away but, at the end of the day, it wasn't my dog, it was Anne's. I just hoped that Anne would have the resources to look after the puppy and be kind to her.

Two weeks later, Anne came to my shop with the dog. She told me she couldn't handle it anymore, and that it wasn't fair to the dog. I asked her if she wanted any money for the dog, but she didn't and merely insisted I take her. She said the dog was wormed and had been to the vet before she'd bought it. She was about to leave, when I called her back and gave her forty pounds to get some food, or booze, or whatever she wanted. Anne said her goodbyes and started tearing up, so I hugged her. I could smell the earth on her damp clothes, along with the smell of cigarettes and booze. She hugged me back, before turning and leaving me with this bundle of black and brown fur with a white spot on her chest and the biggest brown eyes. She was definitely sent to me and, even though a dog was the last thing I needed at this time in my life, I knew she would become my best friend and biggest support.

After I'd been to the vet to clean her up, I took her home to the kids, who were two and a half years old. I called Casper and told him what had happened. I had no idea where he was, but he agreed to present the dog in an open bag, surprising them. He thought I was absolutely nuts for saving her, but it was already too late. I was at home with the children when the doorbell rang. Casper stood outside with the bag, and the kids noticed it moving. Next, there was a head poking out and, my god, the kids were immediately love-struck. It was one of the most beautiful connections I had ever seen. Magnus, in particular, bonded with this dog in such a huge way. I know now that the kids had created a secret language with Rosie, and the three of them understood each other completely. It reminded me of my connection to my dog Laura when I was a kid. Their shared world was far away from the adults' messy world, and Rosie was the best and softest therapist the kids could ever need. Deep down in my heart, I was completely sure that Rosie was sent to me as an angel. In the years that followed, she did her job so well that I simply don't know what I would have done without her. Rosie was gentle with Pepper – she always looked at my daughter with a soft face, no matter how much Pepper tried to tumble with her, and never growled. Magnus, on the other hand, Rosie was rough with. They play-fought, and Rosie would pull his socks off with her teeth, though she never once bit his toes by accident. It was like she knew from very early on that she was going to be a big part of growing these kids up. Her role was to keep them safe, and she performed it admirably. She was always loyal, soft, ever-so-kiss-able, and a very good listener, even to my endless exclamations of, "Why? Why? Why?"

I fought for the shop's survival, the recession was lurching around the corner after all, and asked Casper every day to look for a job to bring some money in, as the shop was carrying all our expenses. I suggested he could be a truck driver again, a bus driver, anything – but he just didn't want to look. He didn't want to be away from his kids on some truck, and he kept saying the shop needed him. He couldn't handle not having any money and not being the big shot with a big car – it was so important to him, and I learned that, unless Casper felt like people were looking up to him, he would never be a kind man. It brought the worst out of him, struggling as we did. He went into a state of denial, and things got so bad between us that I started blatantly sleeping in the kids' bedroom, no longer using their bedtime story as an excuse.

Jumping off the Cliff

In December, 2008, the recession was formally announced in the UK and, within months, we lost all our contracted work. Our real income fell by thousands of pounds, and we had to get rid of the two girls we'd hired to work in the shop, which meant I had to work more myself. It also meant that I had to deliver the kids at eight in the morning and pick them up at six. Not only was this heart-wrenching, but it also meant that I had to deal with the constant media headlines about working mums neglecting their children, and the mums at nursery, who had the same opinion. Of course, they never bothered to ask me whether this was my choice, or whether I was just trying to survive.

Months had gone by, and Casper and I were barely functional. There was no closeness, either mentally or physically, and I spent all my love and energy on the kids and Rosie. Whatever I had left went into trying to save the business. I started to suspect that Casper was up to no good and was lying about his whereabouts, but I was in a place where I just couldn't be bothered. I was too exhausted to pick fights with him or try to figure out what he was up to. At the end of the day, we had kids, and I trusted him to have some self-control, as he had small babies to look out for. If he was any kind of man, he wouldn't jeopardise their futures.

Two days a week, I had half-days at work, as Polly was now working half-time. These days were always packed with doctor's appointments, shopping, admin, or just simply trying to get some time in with the kids. Magnus and Pepper were nearly two and a half years old, by now. One day, I had to drive to the doctor's to get the kids vaccinations, and Casper was going to join me. After collecting the kids, I noticed our van parked outside a very beautiful and posh house. I was happy, knowing that it was probably a big delivery Polly had arranged in the shop.

Once we were in the nurse's clinic, Pepper had her injections first, and Magnus nearly escaped when he saw the nurse poking Pepper to tears. The two nurses and I were running around the room in circles, all the while braving kicking legs, fighting arms, and screaming. It was a circus. Ten stickers for being brave later, I left the clinic, looking to the other parents in the waiting room, who had all heard the circus. With their kids now fearfully hiding under their armpits, the other parents weren't amused with me. The looks said everything, and I ran out of the clinic.

When I tried to get hold of him, Casper still wasn't back, and he wouldn't answer his phone. Coming out of the doctor's office, I had two screaming, red-faced kids on my shoulders, with snot dripping down both of their faces. They were very angry with me after their injections.

Casper came home a few hours later. The kids had slight temperatures, but otherwise were fine – they were already bathed and in bed. He told me he had forgotten about the doctor's appointment. I asked where he'd been, and he said he'd been to speak to a delivery company on the other side of London, to seek work. I knew at that moment that something wasn't right, but I didn't have the strength to ask anything further. I was too exhausted after the day I'd had. I poured a glass of wine and said I'd check on the kids. As usual, I fell asleep. Rosie slept at the kids' feet, and I curled up next to them.

Tom, a very kind and wealthy client, threw a housewarming party at his newest penthouse, and both Casper and I were invited. I was too tired and stressed to consider it, but I said to Casper that I thought he should go and have some fun. I couldn't imagine having to pretend that nothing was wrong with us in front of the party guests. All I really wanted to do was to be at home without him and spend the evening with the kids. At this point, we were communicating only slightly, and all I could think was that his absence would make for the best Saturday night in a long time, as awful as that sounds.

He came home very late. I had texted him several times during the night, asking him where he was. He told me he hadn't been able to get a cab home and he'd had to walk, instead. I was fast asleep when he walked in and, in the morning, I made him breakfast in bed, as I felt bad for abandoning him. As big a prick as he could be, I had this constant feeling that it shouldn't change who I was or how I acted. I knew I'd been very stand-offish and cold lately and, because I've always been quite a people-pleaser, I felt guilty.

At this point, I felt no suspicion – nothing at all. The van in front of the posh house had left my thoughts. He was his usual self and we ploughed on, trying in vain to communicate. I handled the home front almost on my own, and he became more and more slack at the shop, taking ages to deliver flowers and often seeing his mates during work hours.

New Year's Eve was just around the corner, and with some optimism found at the bottom of my soul, I decided to invite over our best friends, Polly and Chey. I had cooked a beautiful lamb, wine was being pulled from ice buckets, and we were choosing old Motown songs and dancing for hours. All of our children were with us. Liam, Polly and Chey's son, was only a toddler, with freckles all over his face. The kids got along, as toddlers do. We were setting off fireworks, and it took my mind back to Denmark, where we used to have huge firework displays on New Year's Eve. Rosie had crawled into the bedroom because of the loud explosions and was lying under the duvets, thinking the human race was ending over the course of one night.

As we were all about to go to bed, Casper told me he was going to walk the dog. It was one in the morning, but I didn't think too much of it. I was a bit drunk and started cleaning up the dishes. Casper left and, after I finished washing up, Polly, Chey, and I decided to have a nightcap. We sat on the couch and waited for Casper to come back. Nearly two hours went by, and I started to get worried. I was sure something had happened, and Chey and I went out to look for him while Polly stayed to look after the kids, who were fast asleep. At this point, I was panicking and thinking of all the idiots on the streets on New Year's Eve. I must admit, I was more worried about Rosie than Casper, but still, he was the father of my kids. We walked around for half an hour, with no idea of where to look, before going back home, where we sat and waited, talking about what to do. Chey tried to calm me down, saying he'd probably met a mate and was having a few beers. While sitting in the lounge with Chey, Polly had fallen asleep with the kids upstairs. Casper suddenly turned up, covered in mud. He told me he'd had to go and look for the dog, as she'd run away after being frightened by the fireworks. He'd searched for her for hours in the woodland surrounding Richmond Park. We all believed him and thought no more of it – we were all just relieved he was safe, and I was relieved that Rosie was safe.

The next morning, Casper was in a great mood and was brilliantly nice. He walked Rosie with the kids and cooked breakfast. I remember looking at Polly and mouthing, 'What the fuck is happening?' She shook her head, aware of all the problems we had. The day went on, and small seeds of hope were planted inside me. Maybe I could find my way back to loving him, or at least just liking him.

I was still debating how to carry on with the business, or whether it would be better to find a job that could cover our expenses. The house still wasn't worth selling, and my relationship with Casper was the last thing I was worried about. We were engaged, and I knew we'd have to fix things at some point, but nothing had changed. From New Year's morning into the next few days, he'd been in a good mood, but that had been a special occasion, and Casper soon went back to not lifting a finger and having grumpy rants at all three of us, as if we were in the way of his happiness. The following weekend, he went out for a few beers, which is something he did really well. I was happy to have Saturday evenings without him, so it was a bonus for both of us.

That night, he didn't come home and didn't text, and I became really worried that something had happened to him. I kept texting but got no response. Yes, we had issues, but the thought of something happening to him frightened me to death. What would I tell the children? I might have been exhausted and drained by his behaviour, but I wasn't a stone-hearted bitch who didn't care about him. In the morning, I frantically called several friends, hospitals, and police stations. We'd been planning on going to the Natural History Museum with the kids and our friends, and he still wasn't home at nine o'clock. He'd never been this bad. I remember the Natural History Museum clearly as we'd agreed to try to do more family stuff in an effort to somehow reconnect. I'd wanted to see if I could like him again, and if he could start acting as an adult. It was funny; I didn't once doubt his feelings for me.

I sat on the sofa while the kids asked where he was. I just told them that Daddy was working and would be home soon. I spoke to Polly on the phone, and she gave me the inevitable, "Do you think he's at another woman's house, sleeping it off?" We'd already established that he wasn't at any mate's house, and I'd called all the nearby hospitals – it hit me suddenly that this could be a possibility. I told Polly that I'd call her in an hour, if nothing changed.

Thirty minutes later, I heard the key in the door, and he walked in. It was ten in the morning, and I walked into the hallway to see him. The kids were playing on the living room floor, on a blanket, with all their Lego pieces. He closed the door gently, as if we were still asleep, and he didn't want to wake us up. His clothes were creased, and his hair was messy. His face looked swollen from drinking, and I noticed scratches on his neck and face. For an instant, I thought he'd been in a fight, but then he looked at me, straight in my face, and I knew. His whole face looked like he'd shagged someone. The guilt was obvious from his eyes, which were blinking nervously, and his body language was telling me that he'd done something wrong. Instead of telling me porkies about where he'd been, he was silent. His hands were shaking, and he walked into the living room and kneeled down to see Magnus and Pepper. They greeted him with kisses and cuddles, oblivious to what he'd done. My gut was doing backflips, and I started trembling. I knew this was it, but I said nothing. All I could think about was how I hoped he'd had a shower before coming home and touching the kids. I couldn't bear the thought of any woman's perfume, or worse, being rubbed on them.

Several thoughts went through my mind: how I'd loved him once, the betrayal, the engagement. The thought of me being worried about him lying in a ditch by the river, and all the while, he'd been shagging someone else, I was sure of it. My intuition told me he had. I wondered if he'd ever thought about his kids through the whole ordeal. I went to the kitchen and started cleaning up after the kids' breakfast. He stayed in the living room, playing with them the entire time. He knew that I knew, and the typical Casper way was to not talk about it and ignore what was happening, hoping that maybe it would just all go away. I finished cleaning and walked upstairs, where I very calmly phoned Sam to say we weren't coming to the Natural History Museum. We'd been supposed to meet Sam, Paul, Camilla, and Steve, the old gang, but I was still shaking. When she asked me why, it was as if she'd pressed a button inside of me and I burst out crying, telling her that Casper had been fucking someone else all night and was very tired and needed some sleep.

"As you do," I sarcastically blurted out. I told her I'd take the kids to Richmond high street instead, and buy them stuff they didn't need. I was completely irrational, and Sam wasn't really sure what to say.

"Okay, well, I'll tell the others you're not coming. I hope it all goes well. Can I do anything, or shall I just give you space?" she said, and it was her way of telling me that she couldn't deal with it. It hit me that, at this point, they were fed up with my chaos and were distancing themselves from me.

"Yes," I answered, "I need a new fucking life."

I calmed down and asked her to lie and tell Camilla and Steve that I was unwell, which, I said, wasn't completely untrue, considering how my life couldn't have been more messed up, at that point. I hung up after telling her that I'd call later, or she could call me after the trip. I turned around and started looking at the walls in the office, trying to figure out what to do. I decided to go downstairs and listen to my intuition. I walked down the stairs, not caring whether he could see that I'd been crying.

"I've cancelled our trip and I'm taking Magnus and Pepper into Richmond. When I come back, I want you and your stuff gone."

Just like that. He begged me not to leave him, begged me to talk things through, told me it was a one-off, and said it was just someone he'd met in a bar after getting too drunk. *Who the fuck does he think he is?* That was the only thought going through my mind. It infuriated me that he thought I didn't see him for who he was; that he actually thought I was that dumb. Maybe it was my own fault for carrying on for so long.

I ordered him to stay away from the house until I'd figured

out how to do this. I was furious. The strangest thing is, I also felt a huge sense of relief. Here it was, finally, in black and white. No more grey zones. It was pure emotional betrayal, but it was now truly official, and I saw a door opening. I could finally get out of it all. I mean, who the hell spends their life like that? Was it my time to decide not to?

I went to Richmond with Magnus and Pepper, who had no idea what was going on. I went to the toy shop and just whacked loads of stuff on the credit card. I felt numb and badly wanted a stiff drink. I called Kirsten, a close friend in Richmond who had, until now, listened to my problems with Casper. She was a Danish friend I'd met through the shop, and she'd married a multi-millionaire who had then left her bankrupt, both financially and emotionally, with three kids. She was a survivor and remains an extremely spiritual being.

I told her what had happened, and she said, "You shouldn't be on your own, come over to my place. Are the kids okay?"

I answered, "They're fine, they have no clue what's going on," and I felt happy that someone was going to look after me, even if only for a moment. I went to her house in the Alberts, an area built with mews and houses and small roads in Richmond, almost like a little town on its own, just a few minutes away from the high street. I took the kids' bags, along with Magnus and Pepper's hands, and started walking. Arriving at her house, we rang the doorbell and could hear loud barking. She opened the door and her big dog, a Golden Retriever called 'Sonny', greeted the kids by licking them. Magnus started laughing out loud. Kirsten was a tall woman with long, blonde hair, big lips, and blue, almond-shaped eyes. She hardly needed makeup and always looked immaculate in just a t-shirt and jeans, as she was wearing now. The kids ran to her small back yard with Sonny and I went into her kitchen, dumping all the bags on the floor. Her new boyfriend, Aidan, came in to ask if I needed a coffee or a stiff drink. Aiden was of normal height and muscular build, and he was a friend of

Casper's. He always had paint on him and smelled of wood, as he was a furniture decorator and restored old pieces. Through my and Kirsten's friendship, we'd been out on several nights together in the pubs, and he knew Casper well. I started sobbing. Everything came out. All the shit he'd put me through over the last three years; the finances, the shop, his cheating, the mobile sex, the debts. I think I spoke for two hours, nonstop. Aidan came in and put some food on the table, along with more wine. He heard everything but said nothing. Kirsten looked at me and told me I needed to leave Casper. She told me he was making me sick, and that he didn't care about his kids. If he did, he wouldn't have put this financial strain or emotional abuse on their mum, and on our little family.

"Kat," she said to me, "we've known for a while that there's been crazy stuff going on."

So this was why Aidan had been so quiet. I looked at her.

"What do you know?"

"I just know that he's told Aidan he's been flirting with a newly divorced woman." In the midst of it all, my phone kept beeping. I scrambled through my bag to find it. I looked at the phone, and it was Casper, asking where the kids and I were. I switched my phone off.

"Anything else?" I asked Kirsten and Aidan.

"No," she said, "and believe me, if there was, and I didn't know about it, I would pull Aidan's balls off, honey, even though I want another baby!"

I sat there all day, until it turned into evening. I'd texted Polly, and she'd said she would come straightaway, but I'd asked her to look after the shop, instead, as I had no idea when I would be able to stand in the shop and face clients. Polly said she'd make arrangements for Liam, her son, and not to worry about anything, shop-wise.

The kids were playing with their new toys and Sonny, as they watched CBBC. I was quite tipsy by now and switched my phone back on. I phoned Casper and told him that he needed to collect our children and he needed to walk Rosie. He came, and Aidan greeted him, not sure of what to say. They just shook hands. Aidan looked at him as if to say, "I feel sorry for you, mate, but you've gone too far." He looked disappointed in Casper, after everything I'd just told them. Casper looked like he'd been up for days, with me knowing that he'd been fast asleep in someone else's bed. I couldn't have cared less for him. He had massive bags under his eyes and still looked scared and quivering. The kids were happy to see Casper, and I told them that Mummy needed to sit with Kirsten because something had happened and I was a little sad.

I turned around to Casper and said, "I'll be home soon, and when I get home, I want you to leave. I assume you've packed all your stuff and gotten rid of it?"

He looked at me funny, as if he didn't think I'd been serious that morning. He'd messed up so many times, so why should this be any different? What he didn't know was that I was in a different place now, and I'd finally had enough. My fear had turned into survival mode. I knew I couldn't go on like this.

He nodded and said, "You don't think we should talk about it?"

I said, "No, we have nothing to talk about. You've made a choice, and so have I, see you later." I kissed Magnus and Pepper all over their faces. They giggled, and Magnus looked at me as if to say, "Don't be sad, Mummy." Maybe it was the wine, but I felt a desire in my heart to get better from this. I wanted to be a happy mum, not what I was now.

I think it was the first time in months that Casper actually took them home, cooked for them, bathed them, and read them a story. That alone made me nervous, and I realised that my life with him truly was a mess. I had been on my own, for a long time, without facing the facts. Ironically, I had done what Casper always did: ignored it and hoped that the problems might vanish.

That day, I felt like I'd sent the kids home with a babysitter I hadn't used before. I found myself texting Casper how to do the bath and reminding him that Pepper was allergic to Johnson's shampoo.

Kirsten and I went to the pub. Sisterhood kicked in, mixed with the wine. I hadn't heard anything from Sam, not even a missed call. I wondered how their day had been at the Natural History Museum, and if she was worried about me and kids.

My head was spinning, and I couldn't stop thinking about how Casper had shagged some young blonde chick that he'd picked up in a random bar, or who this divorced woman could be. Kirsten and I got heavily drunk, and we slagged men off all night. We were trying to figure out where he would have shagged her: in her bed, or in an alley and then her bed, etc. I realised, as I listened to Kirsten talk, that her relationship wasn't so peachy, either. I felt I had failed on an epic scale, and it dawned on me that I had to start all over, with two kids under my arms. I had no idea of what a relationship was meant to be, anymore. I'd invested so much time in cleaning up all the emotional and financial stuff that I'd forgotten to ask myself what I wanted out of it, in the long run. Kirsten was getting very drunk and asked random men in the bar why they were ruled by a piece of meat dangling between their legs that didn't weigh more than a few grams, and how they could let it ruin other people's lives. Some grinned, some weren't amused, and it was definitely an indicator that it was time to go home.

I came home before the pub closed and found Casper sitting on the couch, looking anxious. All I could think was, *Welcome to my world, motherfucker,* as I'd spent almost our entire relationship like that. I ignored him and I went to the kids' bedroom and lay down on a mattress on the floor. Rosie cuddled up to me and I was, mixed with the crying and the wine and the exhausting talks about why people cheat, flat out within minutes.

The next morning, I woke up around five, the light

streaming in through the window. The first thing I felt was a throbbing headache. On top of that, my head was all over the place, but my feelings were the same. My first thought was that being on my own could actually be a relief, a new beginning, something not to be scared of. However, this feeling was still battling my fear and anxiety. It was strange how adrenaline and alcohol could remove fear. Now, I could feel it slowly creeping back into my body. I just lay there, wondering why I'd spent so much time and energy on being afraid, instead of using that energy for something positive. I was more used to spending energy on negative issues, such as our problems, than working on the positive sides of my life, like where I was heading and what I'd already achieved. If I'd spent the same energy on positive things, would I have been in a different place now? I wondered what a breakup would do to the kids. How could I deal with a broken family and make sure they knew it wasn't their fault? The guilt started creeping up in me. I had to take responsibility for a broken family, and I wasn't sure how to handle the thought of it or, for that matter, deal with it in real life.

I put my face in my hands and cried. I could smell the cigarettes Kirsten and I had bought the night before and smoked all night, and I retched slightly. I got up, looked at Magnus and Pepper sleeping, and felt such an urge to just whisk them away to somewhere safe, away from all this chaos.

I went downstairs, where Rosie came to me and licked my legs. I made coffee, took some aspirin, and sat on the couch for ten minutes before I could deal with the world. Only then did I realise that Casper wasn't there.

I took a shower. It was calming to have the water running over my face, and I stood there for at least thirty minutes before I finally got out. I wrapped some towels around me, poured another coffee, and phoned Polly, who was happy to hear my voice. She had texted me several times to see how I was.

"Stay strong, my love," she said. "He might just not be worth it, you know? Are you okay? How are the kids?"

We spoke for a while, and I felt calm and less alone after chatting with her. After I'd sat there for an hour, staring into the air and feeling emotionally beaten up, I was eventually able to breathe better, but my mind and body were still in total turmoil.

The kids had woken up. They were my emotional blanket. I cuddled them and kissed them good morning, and I knew I had to pull myself together in front of them. I phoned the nursery and told them that both kids were unwell.

Shortly after, the doorbell rang. Casper was standing outside. He had slept in the van and looked like shit, which was something I felt good about. I let him in to say good morning to the kids. I made the kids breakfast, put the telly on, and asked him quietly to come into the kitchen.

"You need to move away from here. Take the van and go."

He turned to look at me and said, "Where to?"

I phoned a friend of mine who had a small boutique hotel, where I did weddings sometimes, and she said it was fine for him to stay, so long as she didn't have to get involved in our personal stuff. I thanked her and put the phone down, then looked at Casper.

"We have a place for you to stay. Please say good bye to the kids and leave."

Casper moved out, and I imagined him feeling sorry for himself, lying there on his own in a small hotel room, without his family. Thinking back, he probably enjoyed the silence and ordered room service while sex-texting random women. And the sad thing is, I also look back and wonder why the fuck I organised it for him. Part of me thinks I should have moved into the hotel and let him stay with the kids, but I didn't trust him to look after them or Rosie.

Days went by, and the knowledge that he wasn't using my money, lying about his whereabouts, or failing to pull his weight made me feel as if a huge burden had been lifted from my shoulders. Why I hadn't left him earlier was a major question too, believe me, but I believe that everything is a process – I needed to reach that point where I could walk away, free of any guilt and safe in the knowledge that I'd tried. He had, for so long, made a mess wherever he went, but I'd stopped sweeping up after him. I was done. I'd been lost in an abyss of not knowing who the hell I was. Losing myself had been a slow, painful process that had happened during the mess of our relationship and me becoming a mother.

After a few days, keeping Casper in the hotel stopped being sustainable, so we turned the small office into his bedroom. We sat down, but I really didn't want to be with him. We decided to work in the business separately; he would do deliveries and Monday contracts, and Polly and I would handle the everyday business. For a while, it worked, and it gave the kids time to adapt. Casper realised, for the first time, that I was serious about leaving him, and when I again mentioned a relationship counsellor, he agreed. I wanted it so we could have an amicable split. We went to one session, but it solved nothing. Relationships and parenthood are meant to be one long negotiation, but there was absolutely nothing between us, and he had no input regarding the kids. He was only feeling the victim. I was just crying all the time in front of the counsellor, mourning the fact my family unit was gone, and he got embarrassed about me and apologised to the therapist. When I was digging a little deeper during the session, I found that I was scared and that I felt like I'd been fighting for the wrong thing, all along. I was mourning my own choices.

Afterwards, we went to a nearby pub to have a beer and talk about the session. I told him I wanted to collect the children, and he said he'd go back to the shop. He asked if I would consider staying together, and I just looked at him like someone had stepped on my face and shook my head.

"Go to the shop, Casper, and help Polly close," I said. I was beyond words. I wondered why he wanted to come back, considering he felt like a victim in our family. Nothing made sense.

I so wanted to meet a man who wanted to shelter, protect, and love his family. I knew it was possible, but my journey had been swallowed up in my great and misplaced belief in Casper. What I had failed to see were all the signs of his insecurities, his emasculation, and his failure to ever take responsibility. He was just like a child. As soon as I felt some insecurity, he would feel good. If I was on top, he had to put me down, either by spending money recklessly or seeing other women. He bore no resemblance to a real man. I had let this toxic person back into my life, again and again, because of feeling lonely and clinging on to a family unit that had never existed. Life was a tricky thing, but I was learning. Something inside me opened up and made me realize that instead of just barging on with what I had, I wanted a different path. It was like a revolution had started inside of me.

In the days that followed, I was upset sometimes, and then there would be other days where I felt empowered for figuring out that the death of my relationship with Casper was the best thing that could have happened to me and the kids. These were the days where it felt like I was coming out of jail and learning to live again. They were also sad days; I felt wounded, and my heart was seared with pain. I had to take responsibility for putting myself in a situation where I had ignored every alarm, but I was evolving, for the first time in a long time, as a person. I had been surviving for such a long time but, now, I was actually moving on to a journey of awakening and towards a path where I wanted to be happy. In aid of that, I started to look for the silver lining of everything that had happened between me and Casper, and in my life.

There were also the days that were a never-ending roller-coaster of questions. *What do I do about our money issues? How will the kids cope with us not being together? How will I cope with Casper*

having the kids on his own when we find a place for him? My brain
would just keep on going.

A few weeks went by, and Casper was in the shop more than I
was. I was determined to pick only one battle at a time, and this
one would be about my kids. I was close to them and wanted
them to feel that I was present in this chaos. When you're
fighting so many things, on so many levels, it's hard to keep
focused – I knew I had to try to take one step up the ladder at a
time. I also had no energy to face clients and answer questions.

I kept the kids on some half-days from nursery to enjoy my
time with them. Rosie was over the moon, and I found some
peace simply by letting go of everything. I surrendered to the fact
that I had no control over what had happened. The level of chaos
was profound, so surrendering seemed like the easy choice. Everything I had tried to hold on to in the past slipped out from
between my fingers.

Walking Rosie in Richmond Park while the kids were in nursery, I got a phone call from Gary, my friend and financial advisor.

"Where are you, Kat? I'm waiting at Starbucks."

I realised I'd totally forgotten that I'd arranged to meet him
there. I wanted to talk to him about all my debts and ask him
whether I could get some equity out of the house to make a clean
break. I wanted to get Casper out of the house, and for us both to
pay off the money we took out on various credit cards and
accounts.

I tried calling Casper to let him know that I was going to the
meeting, but there was no answer. I jumped in the car and rushed
to park opposite Waitrose in the town centre of Richmond. I
passed the shop and saw that it was closed. There was a note on
the door. My heart dropped. Not only were we in financial shit
and relationship hell, but now Casper had stopped our only
source of income. I drove a bit further and saw the van, with its
massive logo, parked outside a pub called 'The White Cow'. I
parked my car further up and called Casper again. He picked up

and told me he was at the shop. I said that we both knew that wasn't true and told him I was going to a meeting with the financial advisor. Finally, I told him to re-open the shop and stop embarrassing us. I slammed the phone down and sat in the car, watching the pub. He came out with some woman, kissing and cuddling, as if that was a normal thing to do. I didn't give her much attention – I didn't know which one of his women this was. I had given up keeping track of what was going on. I started the car and drove past them, beeping the horn, and stuck my hand out of the window with my middle finger up. I felt terribly good, after that. Casper looked angry, and the woman looked down at the ground.

When I met Gary at Starbucks, I was out of breath from running to get there. I greeted him, and he ordered me a coffee. I put what had just happened to the back of my mind, determined to sort my life out financially. Gary said nothing I hadn't suspected – I couldn't get my money out of the house to get rid of my debt, not with the recession. He went on about the financial crisis, which I knew all about. The recession was aired on the news every day, and it had made banks and lenders much more careful. I stopped him and told him what Casper had done. I told him everything – it came rushing out all at once. I told him not to take any of Casper's phone calls or emails. It was, after all, not his mortgage. I told Gary I would call him once I had moved Casper out of my house.

He said, "Kat, I think we've all been waiting for this moment."

I looked at him with my jaw dropped down a few meters and, before I got the chance to reply, Casper stormed in. He told me to never give him the finger like that again.

I looked at him and said, "You're fucking joking, right? You closed the shop to go off snogging another woman, and *I'm* the one being disrespectful?" He put his hand up to tell me to be quiet and gave Gary a handshake. I continued, "I have instructed

Gary not to deal with you, anymore. You're not the one who pays him, and you don't return the money you borrow, so go enjoy a muffin and ask him for advice on how to get a mortgage for the shed you're about to move into." I said goodbye to Gary and left Casper there, red-faced. *Welcome to my world again, Casper.* Walking fast around the corner, not knowing if Casper was going to follow me, I thought about Gary's comment. I was right to leave this man. I felt the adrenaline rise inside me. Something was shifting.

I went to open the shop and tried to breathe normally. What the hell had Casper become? A monster? At six, I went to pick up the children before returning home. Casper was there, waiting for me, but I ignored him. He had nowhere to go.

The next few days passed in a blur. Casper decided to tell me that he'd been having a full-blown affair with an American woman, and that she'd asked to meet on the day of one of our meetings with Gary. He had gone to see her to make her understand that he wanted to try to fight for his family. He didn't ask me if I wanted him back, he just assumed – or maybe he was scared of asking me. By this point, I had no idea where I was. My whole body had shut down – everything but the will to survive.

"So what was all the kissing about?" I asked.

"She was upset, and I felt bad for her."

"Casper, I can't do this anymore. I want it to end."

"I know," he said.

New York, New Dreams, and Woody Allen

⋆❧⋆

A fter a few more days of arguing, Casper decided to play noble and suggested he go to his father's place in Holland to ask him if we could borrow some money. If so, it would allow Casper to move out and get his own place. With the recession now in full swing, sales in the shop were way down, so I was willing to follow him – we needed money, more than anything else. Quietly, I was surprised; maybe he had a fragment of sense, after all. So Casper went off to Holland and we agreed that, upon his return, he would stay in my house until he found his own place. He told me he would call when he had arrived in Holland.

The next day, I took Rosie to Richmond Park after dropping the kids off at nursery. It was a wet, muddy day, and playing with Rosie and her ball, I quickly got covered in mud from the splashes of the puddles and running around with her. It was my hour of forgetting everything that was going on. Rosie was my saviour and kept me from going completely mad. The walks were like therapy. I was about to go back to the car when I realised I'd dropped my keys in the middle of Richmond Park. I was gripped with panic – it would be like finding a needle in a haystack. The flowers for the event were standing ready in the shop – I just

couldn't get to them. It was a huge event at Kew Gardens to celebrate the redecoration of the Prince of Wales Conservatory. My
blood drained. I called Casper's phone, as I knew he had spare
keys for the car, somewhere. No answer. I called his dad, who said
it was lovely to hear from me but, due to the language barrier, we
didn't get far. Finally, he told me that Casper had never arrived
and had never spoken to his father about coming. It was all a lie –
there was no truth to it whatsoever. There I was, covered in mud
from top to toe, a happy wet dog wagging its tail at me, two kids
in the nursery I owed money to, and with no fucking idea what to
do. I owed the shop landlord money, so I didn't really fancy
calling him for a key, and I had no idea where the father of my
kids was. I phoned every friend he had, but they all said they
didn't know where he was. I walked down to the shop, swearing
my head off all the way, looking like a frantic homeless person
with a dog. People walking past me swerved around me or crossed
the street.

Finally, I got a locksmith to open the shop doors, counting my
blessings that my credit card had gone through. I'd left the car by
Richmond Park and would probably get a ticket, meaning I had
to deliver the flowers in a cab.

When the delivery was done, I opened the shop again, and
the dog was fast asleep in the corner, on her blanket. I, on the
other hand, was far from tranquil and started my frantic search
for Casper. I kept calling him and trawled through his bank statements, searching for any withdrawals that could indicate where
he was. In between, I smiled at customers as if nothing had
happened.

To this day, I still don't know how I kept up the charade so
well. None of the customers had any idea of the turmoil inside of
me, but I suppose I couldn't afford to close the shop – pretending
nothing was wrong was my pause button from all the madness.

Back in front of the computer, I finally found some clue as to
Casper's whereabouts. On an online bank statement for our joint

account, I found several entries in US dollars. One entry had him spending money in a New York restaurant called 'Giovanni's', and the name rang a bell. Looking it up online, I saw it was a place I'd been to when travelling with my parents. This was no coincidence. I'd told him about this place and my wish to go back. It was a place where they sang opera and had red leather seats in booths. It had been there for generations, serving famous people like Frank Sinatra and Marilyn Monroe. It had all the stars' pictures hanging on the walls in black and white, pasta dishes were thrown on the table when the chef saw fit to serve them, and red wine was poured whenever a glass was empty. I remember, as a fourteen year old, sitting there between my parents and my mum's work friends, on yet another business-turned-family trip, and just sucking in the atmosphere. It had a special place in my heart, as it was where I started imagining living in New York, especially in *Greenwich Village*. It was like being in *A Chorus Line*, which was a favourite musical of mine, and I always had a desire to go back and become a Broadway script writer or actress after watching it.

New York – my New York, my *Sex and the City*, my Woody Allen movies, my dream of going back to Greenwich Village, my Meryl Steep – he was there to pollute it. I had to hand it to him; it was much more glamorous than me standing in muddy boots, nearly bankrupt, offering nothing in the bedroom, with demanding twins, Rosie, and greasy hair covered in dry shampoo. The story about the American woman had now become a reality, and after putting the puzzle pieces together, it was clear that she was the one he had slept with. The pub incident was to meet up, not to break it off. I was a fool. It was overwhelming how good a liar he was. I got so angry that I smashed pots in the back of the shop and threw vases up against the wall. I started screaming, just screaming. Rosie was looking at me as if I'd lost the plot, which I had, because I was still believing this fucking idiot, thinking he was helping our little family with its financial troubles, and instead he was using the only cash we had. He did nothing but run a narcissistic world of his own. What the hell had I done? I was lucky no customer had walked in and seen me in my despair, but then again, I felt no remorse. I felt good. It was just pots and vases, and I hadn't broken yet.

I texted him, asking 'How is New York?' but heard nothing. I cleared up my mess, realising as I did so that I was symbolically sweeping up after him. I knew it had to stop. I collected the children by bus, cooked them dinner, and just sat at the table, completely raw, eaten up by the lies. It was clear to me that we weren't going to do this together. I was going to have to survive him – but how I'd do that, I had no idea.

The next day, he sent me terrible text messages. He told me I was going crazy, and that he was in Holland. That he still tried to mind-fuck me was unbelievable. After a few abusive messages back and forth, I ignored him. It would have to wait until he came back. I actually didn't care about being right – I cared about how he clearly didn't want to do right by me or his kids.

That evening, after collecting the kids and cuddling them, I felt a sense of peace – I knew I'd caught him again, and that I wasn't going crazy. The clarity of seeing his true nature was better than being in turmoil in my head. I learned slowly that I should keep listening to my intuition. I put the kids to bed after their bath and phoned Polly to tell her about New York. When she picked up the phone and I heard her say, "Hello?" I broke down.

"Polly," I shouted, "he's fucking gone to New York, fucking New York! That's *my* city, so why am I the one standing in shit up to my knees while he's having fun in New York?"

"Love, you will go to New York again, I promise."

She was a soothing blanket on my fragile being. I just started crying, thinking how he'd built me up, how he'd actually made me think he wanted to help us, his family. He could have used a different lie – he could have said he was pissing off on a boys' trip. It was how he'd wanted to make me think he was doing the right thing that indicated his position, which was on the border of insanity and cruelty.

After way too many glasses of wine, I texted him, 'I'm pregnant, by the way, so enjoy the Big Apple and tell whoever you're with that they'll have to be a step mum to three kids, now.'

I went to bed thinking how it would really piss him off or shock him and ruin their trip. Not very sensible, and a really low blow, I know, but I'd run out of things to say to piss him off. I had, in my drunkenness, not considered the fact that we hadn't had sex for ages, so my jibe was sure to indicate that I was hopelessly desperate and had run out of meaningful things to say.

I woke up the next morning and started looking into whether I could close the business. I now knew that Casper was definitely not going to be any help with the business, which he had tried to drain of all its money. The best thing I could do was to get rid of the shop, stop the money haemorrhage he had caused, and stitch up the open wound.

I went to open the shop and a regular client came in and ordered an arrangement. She stared at me as I worked, her eyes almost burning into me. She was dressed in high-end clothes, her hair impeccable. She was everything I wasn't. I was tired, wearing baggy clothes, and had no makeup on. I asked her how she was doing, and she suddenly blurted out that she knew the truth about my partner and his wrongdoings. She told me that his new love was a friend of a friend and that everyone knew they'd met at my client Tom's party.

"I could tell you more, if you wanted," she said. I asked why she was telling me this. She ignored me and continued. "Everyone at the party had a good look at what they were up to on the terrace overlooking Kew – my Lord, they were not shy!"

It all made sense. I hadn't been able to get hold of my penthouse client, Tom, for an outstanding payment, which was unlike him. The smell of her perfume was starting to make me feel sick. She continued to tell me that she knew they were in New York

KATJA BERG

together, and that the woman he'd met, the American woman, was paying for the whole trip. They'd also seen each other on New Year's Eve – apparently, the woman had bragged to her friends, and most of the Richmond Hill wives, that he'd run all night to wish her a happy New Year and then shag her up against a tree so her guests wouldn't catch them.

The woman looked at me, saying, "Kat, she wants your man, and she'll go to any extent to get him. She's a dangerous woman – she doesn't care about you or your kids. She jokes about you, and she's been in the shop several times, just to observe you. It's almost as if she's obsessed with you."

I was about to throw up at the thought of Rosie having to watch them shagging up against a tree. I'd need to buy her a big bone as a reward for surviving that ordeal.

"Who are we talking about?"

"Fiona, that's who. She's in a nasty divorce, at the moment."

"Who is she?"

I didn't know who this woman was, or when she'd been in my shop. Her name was 'Fiona', American, part of the posh clientele, but I had no idea what she looked like. She was divorcing a very wealthy man and had three sons. That's all I knew. While my customer was giving me all the gossip about Fiona and Casper, my mind wandered. Everything fell into place, and I slowly got my mind back. I realised I'd been brainwashed for years by this man. Casper was an utter fake and a pathological liar. He had no filter whatsoever and would go to any length to get away with whatever crime he was currently committing. Maybe he and Fiona deserved each other. I somehow managed to come back to reality, engage with the customer, and finish her flowers.

She finally left, saying, "I'm really happy I told you. No one deserves this treatment, and you've done nothing wrong to Fiona. You needed to know the truth. Your poor children!"

She felt better for telling me that I was the latest victim of housewives' gossip. Her telling me convinced her that she'd had

96

no part to play in this and released her from any guilt of being involved. I thought that I should have charged her more for the flowers, as this was really a therapy session for her.

I, on the other hand, knew for sure that everyone knew, and yet no one had said anything. I knew I had to leave him before I became seriously ill. I wondered whether any of these women could have perhaps pulled each other aside and asked if Casper and Fiona's 'romance', and her behaviour towards me, was an okay thing to witness in silence. Could they not have made a difference by shouting out loud that it wasn't okay? Could the woman who'd followed Fiona into my shop not have said, "Enough is enough"? Why was I a laughing stock? Shag him, but don't be a bitch. Shag him, but don't step on his partner's pride by mocking her and their children. I just kept asking myself, for the rest of the day, why this woman had done this. *What have I ever done to these women?*

I was trembling and wasn't sure how to feel. It was the lies that got to me – everyone fucks up, but his lies had been constant. It was a schizophrenic feeling, and knowing that these women had taken part in Casper's deception made me feel even more protective of my children.

The next day, Rochelle, another client of mine who was also a Richmond Hill wife, came in.

"Hi Kat, is everything okay?" she asked, browsing my selection of vases and pots.

I looked at her – her precise bob, her exquisite skin, and her Miu Miu bag – and was suddenly conscious of my almost see-through leggings, my greasy hair, and my mum jumper.

"I'm good, thanks. How are you?"

Rochelle was a lovely lady who I'd done lots of events with. She was all about charity work and was a stay-at-home mum. She was a good person, but I was on guard, thinking that she might be here to drop another bombshell on my life. I was also asking myself why these women couldn't ever just look like shit for a day, or at least have a broken nail or something.

And then she started in with, "I happened to overhear a conversation in Cedars, the posh gym on the hill – not that I go there anymore; it's full of snobs, and you know I'm not one of those – but I had this pass, so I went in at the weekend."

I was now sure that she felt sorry for me and didn't want to make me feel as if I was beneath her. I might not have been able to afford a gym, but it bugged me that it was an issue for them and made them feel better than me. How a gym membership could give them such an ego was a wonder to me. I could feel that she wanted to get to my level but, in doing so, she was actually offending me.

"I overheard the ladies gossiping about Casper," she said. "They said he's having an affair with this American woman, a mother of three who's currently embroiled in her own divorce settlement. The ladies were laughing so loud at the fact that he was still snooping around. They said that every time they went to buy flowers at your shop, they felt a bit bad, but it wasn't really their business to get involved. Is it true?"

I said, "Yes, it's true, Rochelle, but is it any of your business?"

"Oh god, no, but I just thought you should know. Also, I gave these ladies a dirty look, a stink eye, as they call it, so as to say that I didn't agree."

"Thanks, Rochelle, that was kind of you. Do you need any flowers?"

She bought some flowers, though it was obvious that she didn't need any and wanted to say more. She was twitchy and couldn't stand still as she looked at me.

"My friend, Veronica, came to my house the other day and said she'd seen him at a local Belgian restaurant called 'Brouge'."

Oh god, I thought. We delivered flowers there every week, and I knew the owner well.

"He was standing very close to this full-figured woman,"

Rochelle went on, "and they were almost rubbing up against each other, as if really, they were all over each other, and it seemed very inappropriate. A lot of people were in the same group – a lot of women, in particular."

Again, I wondered where the dignity was for me as a woman, a mother, and a sister. Most of these women were mothers too. Where was the empathy?

"Rochelle, I'm aware Casper is having an affair, thank you for telling me this. The kids and I are having a hard time, but I'm not sure our relationship is at the level where I should be engaging with you about my private life."

She looked at me and smiled, saying, "Of course, don't be silly, I don't want to talk to you about it. I just wanted to tell you what I'd heard. I'm sure you two will figure it out. Let me know if you want me to send any more evil eyes, as I'm good at that, darling." She paid for the flowers, blew me several kisses, and strolled out of the shop. It had been an uncomfortable meeting for both of us, and I was happy to put some distance between myself and these people.

So, on top of losing my income and looking after the demanding kids, I had my partner's affair stalking me into the shop, and apparently, I was the gossip of the suburb. This was a huge change from being a part of the community through my hard work. I was riddled with anger, frustration, and disbelief, and the worst thing was that I had no time to vent these emotions. All I was doing was surviving. My head was buried in papers that explained how to dissolve the company, the kids needed feeding, loving, and comforting, the dog needed to be walked, the house needed to be cleaned, and the shop needed running. Casper, who was seeing the world with another woman, had shattered my credibility. It now seemed like he was the smart one, and I was the one who'd failed to hold the relationship together. After all, I must have done something wrong for him to be out with other women.

Curtains Drawn or Curtains Fall?

After he got back from New York, Casper went straight to Fiona's house. They had both been updated on recent events by the jungle drums of Richmond. Before he came back, I decided to pack all his stuff and place it in the front garden. Very classic – I'd seen it done in every movie about infidelity, but I loved doing it. It felt liberating and cleansing, and I recommend that any scorned woman do the same. I told the kids that I'd found moths in his stuff and it needed airing out, which was completely legitimate!

He texted me after collecting it, 'I will make sure you pay for the stuff that meant something to me – the posters from Holland, the beer labels, the pictures, and more – that is now ruined because it has been out in the rain for three days. That you can be this pathetic is no doubt an indicator of your behaviour problems.'

He'd finally been confronted with all the lies he'd been creating for months, and that was the best he could come up with?

I texted back, 'I will pay for the beer label collection, as I don't want to be responsible for destroying any important memories from your past – that is, when a snowball survives a fire in hell, you prat.'

It was a very low level of communication, I admit, but swearing at him made me feel so good. It was like letting steam out when the kettle is boiling.

Casper took the car, since it was the only thing in his name. I kept the van, but I couldn't drive it, as it was too big. After a week, Fiona helped him find a studio flat and paid for the deposit. They both felt that he had to get away from me, but they also needed to give her sons a chance to get used to the new situation. Magnus and Pepper weren't mentioned in this and weren't considered, either. In the meantime, she was apparently looking for a house to buy with her ex-husband's money. The idea was that, in the interim, Casper could at least live somewhere bearable, instead of with me. The rumour going around was that I was a very angry woman who insisted on creating a toxic environment. It was unbelievable how things got twisted, but I didn't fight it.

I agreed on Casper moving away and yes, I was toxic, but only from all the shit he had filled me with. On top of the rumours, I realised a few days after he moved out that he'd taken a few pages out of the cheque book and paid for a month's rent at the new studio flat. It left me with no money to pay for food or shelter for me and the kids. I kept sending him abusive texts and hitting the lowest notes, but it was the only way I could vent and let him know how disgusting I thought his behaviour was. It was also a desperate call for him to wake up and do the right thing, but it wasn't heard.

It soon became very messy. Casper would come to the shop, and I would instantly leave. Sadly, I had to keep him on as we had no staff left, and I had to collect the children from nursery. Polly had her own son to go and collect, and I could barely afford her. Casper had no idea that I was planning to close the shop. I'd released him as director and, when it came to crunch time, all the papers had been prepared.

Unfortunately, he'd gained confidence from seeing Fiona. She seemed to love him unconditionally, after only a very short time. She judged me for my behaviour and never doubted anything Casper said. Casper would come into the house whenever he wanted and had absolutely no respect for my privacy. I changed the door locks, but he would ring the doorbell until I would open it, again with no regard for the kids. I knew that trying to reason with him would result in endless arguments about whose fault it all was, and that would mean exposing the kids, who I wanted to spare as much as possible.

It became a daily routine for clients to come into the shop and ask if everything was okay. They'd raise their eyebrows or wear smirks on their faces, as if they knew better. I was well aware that Fiona and Casper had been flaunting their newfound love on the streets of Richmond and in pubs, restaurants, etc. It was clear they were an item, but that didn't bother me. What bothered me was the lack of respect from both of them. It was apparently okay for everyone to know what was happening, and my private life was on public display in a small town. Casper started missing his arranged visits and would only see the kids on odd occasions. He was busy being in love and had an active social life. She could afford babysitters and paid for all their outings. He bragged to me that he got a weekly allowance from her, trips paid for, and big parties where the men smoked Cuban cigars and arrived in Jaguars and Porches. Apparently, they all bought his horseshit about having a business in Richmond; my business. He kept blaming me for my terrible business skills and said that was why I was losing everything. It was at this stage that my disbelief turned to numbness. I just kept shaking my head. Soon, everything began to go inwards.

One day, when it suddenly became all too much to bear, I asked him for help – either with the kids or financially. This was when one of his famous and most frequently texted lines was finally uttered face-to-face: "If you can't afford to have the children, I will take them into my care."

I replied, "If you cannot afford to support them now, how can you afford to look after them?"

He said that the offer would continue to stand, but that he didn't want any further interaction with me. I needed not to take my bitterness any further. Of course, there was no way the kids were going to his house, unless it had been agreed upon prior. I didn't understand how he could think the kids would be better off without their mum. They weren't doing great without their dad, but he just kept cancelling. He simply didn't think that childcare was particularly important.

He didn't work – he did nothing. He wasn't even looking for work. He stopped helping me in the shop, except for when he wanted to, which was barely ever. Fiona didn't work either, apart from doing a tremendous amount of yoga. Apparently, she was trying to find her inner yogi, which I found hilarious, considering what she was actively supporting in her private life. She found a six-bedroom house in a fashionable area in Richmond and bought a seven-seater car, as they reportedly wanted to build their own new family, which was to include Magnus and Pepper.

Weeks passed, and the kids didn't see him for nearly three months. He explained his cancellations by telling me that he was having a tough time adjusting to his new lifestyle. Lots had to be put in order, as they were building a new life, which I had to understand was very challenging for them. He had no problems with weekends spent on holiday or socialising at concerts and events, but seeing his kids was too much for him.

I finally broke down and spoke to my parents. I told them how I felt and said that the kids and I wanted to come for a break, and they paid for flight tickets. They had, like me, been waiting for Casper to do the right thing; to make the split, if not amicable, at least dignified, and pull his weight for his children's sake. No such luck, and I was out of breath. Rosie was looked after by Polly, and she was left in charge of the shop, with Casper working the rest of the Valentines rush with her. He had agreed to this, as I would not be present. It wasn't as busy as previous years, as supermarkets had really undercut our prices, and the recession had been unavoidable. Customers weren't looking for quality these days – they were looking for flowers that were red and cheap and kept their partners happy. I couldn't blame them; I was poor myself.

As soon as I landed in Copenhagen, I fell ill. It turned out that I had a terrible ear infection. My sister still lived in the flat underneath my parents', so we were all close. I told no one I was in Denmark, as I couldn't face seeing anyone. My parents took care of the kids while I was ill in bed. I was in contact with Casper and texted him a few times, but I was beaten and had nothing left to say.

My fear of my financial situation was taking hold. It was as if there were two hands around my neck, tightening a little more every day. I stayed in bed for four days, sick as a dog. I was lying in a flat in the middle of my home town, and I didn't see one friend. I think I spent most of the time crying under the duvet.

I came back to England to an empty house, with just Rosie waiting for our return. I opened the door and the sixty kilo furry ball came running towards us. She tumbled with the kids on the living room floor and licked their faces. Their laughter filled the house with warmth again. Polly had left me a note and some food in the fridge. It hit me that she had less money than I did, and still bought me food.

With Casper being absent so long, the kids were starting to wonder. The excuses I'd made, such as, "Let's go on an exciting trip, just the three of us!" and, "Daddy has to work lots," had begun to crumble, and they'd started asking for their dad. I lied for them, so that they wouldn't have to experience the toxic environment between me and Casper. I contacted him to say that we needed to figure out a way for him to see the kids and to spare them from too many changes – by which I meant that he should see the kids without Fiona, so that they didn't get confused. This suggestion was to become my most exhausting battle with these two human beings, Fiona and Casper, and also the one that was most misinterpreted. It seemed they thought I couldn't accept that Casper had moved on, which was just so untrue. I was trying to be an adult and protect the children while putting my own needs aside, giving our kids the same chance they were giving her kids. Casper and I had been done for years. He refused, and Fiona emailed me to say I should move on, and that she was sad to know that my love for Casper was being sent through the kids. I didn't respond and instead went to bed.

I went back to the shop the day after we'd returned from Copenhagen. Polly told me that the shop had done reasonably well and that she'd hidden some cash in a pot in the shop, knowing our full situation. The rest had gone with Casper, but many clients had paid by card, so at least the damage was managed.

I walked into the shop, and any feeling of achievement faded. My achievement of being a successful florist, a successful mum, and a successful partner; any success that meant doing something that made me happy and doing it well. My kids had a split family, a broken woman as a mother, and absolutely no money. I sat on the floor and began to sob. It took me a long time to scrape myself together. I called my accountant and told him to start the legal procedures to close the shop down, then opened the shop and reduced the prices of my stock. The only thing to do now was to clean it out slowly.

Casper still hadn't seen the kids, and I asked him if he would take them swimming. He agreed but, as always, later on in the day, I got the text: 'Hi, I can't collect the children due to some work I might have found.' He was lying through his teeth, but I had stopped arguing. I took the kids instead. I drove past the house Fiona and Casper had moved into on my way back from swimming, and there was the van, with my big fat logo on it. He still had it from the Valentines work. I had the car, and we were about to swap back again as he claimed it was 'all he had left'. The kids were asleep in the back seats and, out of nowhere, a devil came up in me. I parked the car in front of Fiona's house and rang the doorbell. She opened it and nearly shat her pants, by the look of her expression. She had a towel around her and wet hair with smudged mascara.

"Can I speak to Casper, please?" I asked. It was the first time I'd seen her, and I was so angry that when she closed the door, I couldn't remember what she looked like. I could hear hard, loud footsteps on the stairs.

Casper came down and opened up the door, still zipping his fly as he said, "Kat, you shouldn't just show up here."

"You're right, Casper, I just needed to catch you lying again, or did the job interview involve you having to put your dick in the interviewer's mouth? Impressive, really, as I know that your dick has been in a lot of places."

I knew that Fiona would be listening, and it was the most horrible thing I could come up with. He shook his head and told me I was an embarrassment to the kids.

"The kids are called 'Magnus' and 'Pepper', in case you've forgotten, and they're asleep right now, but maybe you want to take a picture, so you won't forget what they look like, you piece of shit."

I turned around, went back to the car, and drove off. He texted me later saying that, if I showed up at the house again, Fiona would call the police. He didn't ask how his kids were. I didn't reply. I just left it, wondering what had made me do it.

I decided to take the van back, which he returned with loads of old flowers in the back. It was a clear message that I was still to clean up after him. After all the years I'd spent nagging him about finances, he'd developed an urge to put me down. There was no logic to it, and I didn't react to it. I just cleaned out the van.

As I couldn't drive the van, I had to take the bus every day to get the kids to nursery. It was challenging with two little toddlers, although I didn't mind. Believe it or not, though, the bus didn't allow buggies at rush hour, which made it difficult. My work demanded that I get a car so that I could do deliveries in the morning and evening, so I had to get rid of the van and look for a car. The van had been bought on a financial agreement, and it turned out that, with this kind of agreement, when half of the money is paid out, you can then return it to the bank. I would be left with no van, but also no debt on it to pay, so I did. This left me with no money to buy a car. I asked Kirsten if she could help. She told me her cleaner's husband, Leon, could help me get a second-hand car. He was from Columbia and had experience in car trading. He called me and told me to meet him at Roehampton Lane, as there was a car there he had already looked at. It was £840, and he had test driven it. I asked my parents again to borrow money, and they, of course, helped me. I went to meet him a few days later and found him by the car with a Chinese guy. I took it for a test drive and it seemed fine, though I had no clue about cars.

The Chinese guy said, "Good car, £840 deal, man."

I answered, "Can we consider eight hundred? I'm really struggling, it would be a great help if you could."

"No deal, woman. £840 or get out of my car."

I gave him the money, got the papers, and was suddenly the proud new owner of a blue Nissan from 1986. Leon shook my hand and I thanked him, promising that I would put aside some flowers for his upcoming wedding. I drove away with shaky legs. I was in a new world of complete abandon. I had a new car on a new road, and I had no clue what the next step was.

One Door Closes and Another One Opens

I n April, 2009, I made the tough but sensible decision to hand
back the keys to the shop lease owner. I'd been in the shop
for five years and made some good money, but I was running the
risk of losing more than I had made if I didn't get out. I was sad,
but I was looking forward to spending more time with my kids
and not carrying the weight of running the shop on a daily basis.

The business had been sinking, and sinking fast. I owed
£10,000 in shop rent, and I didn't have a penny on me. I was
living on credit cards, and Casper had just emptied out our joint
account buying Calvin Klein – yes, underwear. The bank statement clearly showed it in black and white. He'd gone to the same
shop in Richmond where the clerk had told me that my tits were
too saggy for a certain bra style that I liked. I could have cried.

My lease didn't include a break clause for the time I wanted to
leave, so I had to beg the landlord to let me go. I was doing all
this on my own, and while Casper was bragging about his business to his new love and new friends, I was dissolving it. The
landlord was quick to threaten to take me to court for money
owed. I told him, "Good luck," as I had none. I emptied the shop
of the things I loved and gave the keys to the son of the landlord,

who was quite decent about everything. Not realising what the recession had done to everyone, the landlord himself carried on, threatening me with legal action. I wished him well. For five years, I had paid over £100,000 in rent. I had no energy left. I had bigger battles to fight.

After I'd given the keys back to the landlord, I felt a surge of relief for a short moment. I could now focus on just surviving, instead of trying to figure out how to pay the next flower bill or rental payment. Of course, I didn't know how I was going to carry on, but at least this was a new fear and a different direction. It already looked like it offered more options.

All my stuff from the shop was moved into storage, and I had all my office supplies in my living room. One night, when the kids were asleep, I sat in the living room, which had no furniture, as Casper had taken it all for his studio flat, I looked outside at my rusty blue Nissan, and then back at all my papers on the floor, and I just started sobbing. Sad, lonely, penniless, full of anxiety, riddled with debt, drinking glasses of wine in a mug a friend had given me... I just sobbed. I had no idea how I'd ended up here. Rosie laid her head on my lap. It was warm, and her breathing calmed me. She was looking at me with her brown eyes, as if to tell me I wasn't on my own. I fell asleep next to her, surrounded by unopened brown letters labelled with red writing.

Unfortunately, things started getting even more ugly. Fiona was determined to get involved. I think she felt as if she was protecting Casper from me, the toxic and bitter woman. She thought I was the reason he was where he was. I understood why he was with her; he got unconditional love, protection, warmth, care, and admiration. His aim was to be loved without loving, and he had surely succeeded. Casper was deceptive – he got women to believe he loved them, and then he would stop loving you and use you instead. I was glad to have gotten rid of him. I felt sorry for Fiona, but she made it easy for me to forget this; I'd receive emails from her at two in the morning where she'd go on about how little Casper had in his life, and if I could just, for once in my life, not emasculate him and let him have his way and blah, blah, blah.

I tried many times to arrange for Casper to visit the kids at my house. I planned to leave while he was there, so as not to confuse the twins. He completely refused this and still believed my intention was to punish him for falling in love with someone else.

He said, "Kat, you need to let me go and get on with it. I love Fiona – please accept this."

I would reply, "Why not try it a few times, and then you can start taking them to yours – I just want to ease them into it."

"Kat," he'd say, "please don't let the bitterness affect the kids."

It was just impossible for me to figure out a way to make this a gentle transition. It was Casper and Fiona's way or the highway. She had bought the house, he had moved in, the seven-seater had been purchased, and they were all set to be a family. They called her three kids Magnus and Pepper's brothers, and this was after only four months of knowing each other, right from when they first shagged at Tom's party. Casper said that I made it too diffi-cult to see the children and hardly saw them. I told him he could take them out on day-trips, for dinner, to birthday parties they had been invited to, but each offer was declined with the same response.

"Please, Kat, move on. The kids will be fine, and I will see them in good time. I am their father, and I'm adjusting my life so they can have a great one."

My reply lowered the tone, somewhat.

"Go fuck yourself, douchebag."

I kept pushing him to see his kids, and he kept accusing me of not letting him go emotionally. I kept going because I knew this was about the kids and not me. I felt it was my responsibility, as their mother, to try to the point where nothing else could be done. Finally, we slowly arranged for him to visit the kids. The result of us not being able to agree was many cancelled days and swapped weekends, but at least he was finally seeing them.

Of course, he went against my will and introduced them to Fiona. He had picked them up on a Friday from nursery, as arranged, and had taken them to her house, with her sons, instead of on a weekend away, as I had prepared them for. I hadn't been warned, so I knew nothing before the kids came back to tell me. Predictably, the kids were confused; weeks went by, and after lots of hard work, I got the kids to understand that it was okay for Mummy and Daddy not to be together and for Daddy and Fiona to be together. It's ridiculous that I had to talk to three-year-old kids about this.

One day, he came to collect the children and told me I had put dirty clothes on them to embarrass him. I stared at him.

"What? Why would I do that?"

The kids were standing between us in the doorway, listening to all of it.

"Because you're trying very hard to make my life with Fiona difficult."

I was completely dumbfounded. His ridiculous accusations continued, and he was backed up by his doting new girlfriend. I ended the conversation. The kids were there, and it felt wrong to expose them to our anger.

I'd suggested that, after recent events, I come see their house with the kids to show them there was no hostile situation, which was obviously a total lie. Deep inside, I wanted to grind their faces in cow shit for the grief they were putting my kids through. The idea of a comforting and secure relationship with their father as a foundation for our mess had gone. I wasn't allowed to meet Fiona's three sons, who were playing with the twins and who were their 'new brothers', and I wasn't allowed to see the kids' room, where they ate, or even come in the house. It was a decision they had made and thought was best for all involved. It was an absolute farce of a new relationship. Fiona didn't want me near her or her sons, but felt fine taking my twins and creating a relationship with them. Casper applauded this.

I was completely blocked out, whenever I tried to reason with them. I kept reminding them to ask themselves, "Is this the best thing for all the children involved, hers and ours?" The reply was always the same. It was like the feeling you get when you're finished throwing up and then still have to heave. After a while, I gave up trying to explain it to them. I had been warned by friends who had been in similar situations not to refuse to let him see the children, as this would play against me if I was ever taken to court over custody and, worse, affect the kids to see their mum denying them access.

In the beginning, with the kids going to their place on some weekends (when he didn't cancel), it was like having an arm cut off. The house was quiet, and it felt unnatural to be without them. I felt riddled with guilt over the whole thing and forced into a situation, with the kids, of saying goodbye at the door and them turning and looking at me, not understanding why they weren't saying goodnight to Mummy that evening. It was the feeling of going against everything inside of me. I had to accept that Casper was their father and, to a certain degree, I had to believe he would do the right thing for his kids.

Casper then proposed that the kids should spend five days with him, and five days with me. I thought it would be the most schizophrenic upbringing you could give a kid, and told him, "No way, where would the kids' home base be? When are they meant to say, 'Oh, I'm finally home'? How are we going to organise their social lives? Have you ever tried to live in two places? It's a ludicrous idea."

"You're holding on to something that is gone, Kat," he said, and the conversation ended. I shook my head. I had been here before.

He collected the kids on the Friday after our discussion. We agreed for him to return on the following Sunday, but he didn't arrive. I texted him and called him – no answer. I drove to the house, but no one was home. I was petrified and began to shake. It was now eight in the evening, and their bed time. I called Polly, Kirsten, my parents, my sister... even Sam, who said I should calm down, thinking I must be overreacting to interrupt her day. I was frantic, and everyone else told me to call the police. My parents were going crazy, and my father wanted to take the next flight over. I knew Casper wouldn't hurt them, he loved himself too much to get in trouble like that, but I was worried, nonetheless. What if he kept them? How were they, what was he saying to them, were they wondering why they weren't coming home? I cried, I screamed, I paced around my house and started talking to Rosie, who looked at me as if she was watching a tennis match, her head going left and right. I felt as if I'd let the kids down. My head was exploding over all of the last few months' pressures and compromises, all with someone I'd started to hate so much for the things he'd done and was still doing. In the end, I called the police, who offered to send two officers to my house. They explained that, if it was against an agreement Casper and I had made, and I could prove so with texts, he had officially kidnapped the children. I could, and the police called both Fiona and Casper and explained the situation. They had been out eating in a restaurant and tried to explain that we'd agreed to five days. The police officer who had dealt with me explained kindly that he had seen the actual agreement, and they had two choices. They could either return the children themselves immediately, or they would be collected by the police. Finally, the kids were returned. Casper drove up to the front of the house and let the kids run in themselves. Magnus and Pepper were tired but very happy to see Rosie and be home. Casper couldn't even face me, and he drove off without a word. The police officers had left already, explaining that if he didn't return, I could call the station, and they would handle the situation.

I took a lot of emotional abuse from both him and Fiona later that evening. He told me he'd wanted to keep the kids for five days to prove to me that it would be fine. It was only when I phoned the police that it all went bad, and I had to take the brunt for what I'd just put the kids through and be ready for his next step. I was mystified by how delusional the man was. I stuck Pepper and Magnus in the bath while Rosie watched them, as she always did when the kids were in the bath, to make sure they wouldn't come to harm. I washed their hair, brushed their teeth, and snuggled them under the duvets in my bed, with Rosie lying next to us, on the floor. I was still shaken and kept waking up during the night, checking that they were still lying next to me.

A few days later, the doorbell rang at seven in the morning. Casper stood there, papers in hand. He had decided to prepare documents for court, and Fiona totally agreed with him. He handed them over, his hands shaking.

"Kat, I'm sorry to give you this, but if you just did what I said, it wouldn't have to come to this."

With that, he turned and left. He didn't ask to see the kids and say good morning, or ask how they were.

The papers were homemade, intended to look like official court papers – I assumed Fiona thought they could get away with this after learning what such documents looked like in divorce court. All I could think was that they were trying to intimidate me. I took precautions and contacted my lawyer. She recommended a solicitor who specialised in family affairs.

She laughed and said, "Kat, this will be over swiftly, the man is a prat. Don't worry about a thing."

I was still mortified that it had come to this. I had no idea what was ahead.

Getting Lost in a Room

So, without questioning Casper's intentions, and with little regard for the domestic arrangements already in place, the bureaucrats pulled me into court. The family lawyer, who was also trained in child residence cases, taught me that using the word 'custody' was no longer allowed, as it is politically incorrect. This still makes me laugh. I found out later that these lawyers had all been trained to pull a certain number of hours from a client by using a combination of their skills and what I would call emotional abuse. After all, you don't say 'no' to your lawyer if there's a risk of you losing your children. There was no political correctness, there. My solicitor's bills ended up at £35,000. My parents spent their entire pension on them. I thought about the women who don't have the same support system, and realised how lucky I was.

My lawyer was based in Kingston. Her office had glass walls and a swanky table with posh chairs tucked beneath it. In the middle of the table was a tissue box. I remember thinking that I was definitely going to use my share of those, considering how much these people charged. I was asked to sit down and wait for the lawyer. I remember seeing this tiny person on the other side of the glass. She was walking really fast and wearing a black suit, white shirt, and small glasses. Her strawberry blonde hair was cut in a bob. She looked like she had just come out of high school. She came in with a file in her hand and sat down, at which point she began speaking very softly.

"My name is Karen Hansen. I have worked for LML Solicitors for a few years and specialise in family law. How are you, Kat? Why did it come to this?"

"I don't know," I answered. "Because he's a prat who's met an even bigger prat?"

"I'm going to warn you that you'll have to do things you won't like, and you also need to stop using that kind of language. We need to find a way for you guys to work on this, but you'll both need to be willing to do so, and being angry that he's moved on isn't going to help."

I sighed and looked at her for a few moments, as her suggestion was completely transparent.

"Please, don't put me in the 'scorned woman' category. I'm not trying to get revenge on my ex."

I glanced around the room and wondered why this cliché kept coming up, hoping the meeting wouldn't last too long. Which women are to blame for creating this attitude and assumption? Why don't we look after each other more, as both sisters and mothers? *Look a little deeper before you judge, that's all I'm saying.*

I couldn't understand why Fiona and Casper were ready to turn the twins' world upside-down. Why couldn't we agree that the least we could do would be to let the kids recover from our mess, slowly, before throwing this new 'family concept' into their lives?

I was forced to fight to have my kids stay with me, and for them to see their father on a regular, but organised, schedule. I wasn't being unreasonable. Karen told me about the fees and laws, and introduced me to mediation and lots of other things that all cost money. As much as the system wanted to do the right thing, it was obvious that I was standing in front of an abyss of sharks, and they all stood to make money on cases like these. Although I liked Karen, she was part of this.

We went through Casper's demands. He still wanted the kids five days on and five days off. Because the twins were so young, they couldn't actually speak up and say how this situation made them feel, but my attitude hadn't changed. There was also another huge factor: my solicitor pointed out that, should Casper's model be adopted, he'd be released from making child maintenance payments. At this point, he still hadn't supported us financially, at all. Finally, something I understood about his actions; it was about the money, not the kids. Fiona would be paying for them, of course, but having to make payments to me every month would simply be too painful for him. Karen continued to point out that she would, with my agreement, contact them and see if they had appointed an attorney, or were acting on their own behalf, as their papers indicated. I agreed and signed the contract. I stayed there for approximately two hours, talking about the struggles, recent events, and what I wanted from it all. It all boiled down to me wanting Casper to do the right thing for his kids, and Karen explained that this would be the hard part, because we already had all the indications that that wasn't his intention. The potential of what could happen was limited, and I should be prepared for a struggle. She was good at her job and firm in tone.

"Kat, by the end of this, you will be okay, but more importantly, we need to make sure Magnus and Pepper are, as well."

I went home after my meeting with Karen and felt less alone. All we could do was wait for their reaction to me hiring a lawyer. Casper still didn't try to see his kids and kept changing dates on weekends. If I had plans, he'd say, "You can't tell me what to do, anymore, and you should be staying at home with your kids, not going out drinking with your friends," and the stupidity would continue. I simply gave up on trying to go out and was under the spell of Fiona and Casper's plans, as it made it less confrontational for me, and less disappointing when I'd made plans and needed to cancel them because of him rescheduling.

Casper and Fiona hired a lawyer, and eight weeks later, the court procedures started. The family court in Holborn was a big building. I'd taken the tube, and my stomach was all twisted. I met with both my lawyer and barrister outside. My barrister was young and very good looking. *He definitely has manicures*, I thought to myself, as I shook his hand. Karen gave me a hug and asked how I felt.

"Nervous," I replied.

They were both dressed up in suits. I was wearing a dress – size eight, as I hadn't been able to eat much. Unfortunately, I was too nervous and couldn't even enjoy it. That's the downside of losing weight in a broken relationship. Inside, we walked through an entrance hall and passed through a detector. It all felt so surreal. Karen told me that, in court, Casper would be referred to as 'the applicant', and I would be 'the respondent'.

Through all of this, I had still been working eighty hours a week; I'd been trying to salvage the business from home, via online orders from new and existing clients, all while sitting on my living room floor. At the same time, I'd been slowly discovering that Casper had emptied all our accounts, including the children's savings account, which paid for their nursery. I reminded myself, in a stunned silence, that I wasn't allowed to mention this in court, because it would be politically incorrect. Not paying for your kids' food and clothing was, in my mind, negligence, or at least stealing from them on another level. Had I not provided shelter, food, and clothing, social services would have charged me with negligence, and the children most likely would have been taken away and given to their father. It was ironic, to say the least. I was trying to figure out the logic in this, and how privileged Casper's situation was to not fall under the same bracket as me.

I was put into a waiting room with other people in similar situations. I was so scared that I could hardly swallow my own saliva. I wondered whether I should go to the toilet and spit, as my mouth was full. I decided against it, worried that someone would call my name while I was away, and the judge would charge me with contempt of court. Instead, I sat there shaking, playing over the possible scenarios in my head. In front of me were a woman, her translator, and her lawyer. I heard things such as, "He shouldn't see the children, as he tried to kill you," and, "I hope the judge sees sense."

Mr. Harris, the barrister, and Karen sat next to me. They warmed me up by saying that it was normal to be nervous. Karen asked me to let her and the barrister run over my programme for requested contact with the father, as well as the diary I had kept of Casper's cancelled visits. She told me that, even though I was the respondent, I shouldn't respond to anything Casper or his lawyer said, as to do so would create chaos. That was why Mr. Harris was present.

Finally, we were called into court over a speaker phone by a crackling voice with a German accent. On our way, we passed the room Casper was in with his lawyer, where he was sitting at a table. Fiona saw me and walked up to the doorway. She was wearing a short leather skirt and black leather fuck-me boots. She stared at me with a massive smirk on her face. Her hair was blonde, blow-dried by a hairdresser, and she had a crooked nose. It was only the second time I'd seen her, and it took me back. *Who are you, and why are you doing this to me and my babies?*

Karen grabbed my arm and rushed me away, explaining that in family residence court, nobody but family members could be present. This was why I'd come alone, although Polly had wanted to come, and Kirsten was ready to meet me at Richmond train station, on my return. The barrister, who was visibly agitated, asked me if I wanted to dismiss the court visit due to Fiona's presence. I chose to continue, as I couldn't afford to return. Casper and Fiona had just confirmed that this wasn't about the kids, for them. It would have been about the kids if they had treated the case with the sensitivity it deserved, but this was about them versus me. Here she was, ten months after they'd begun their affair, looking like a parody of the big-busted woman from the movie *Liar Liar* with Jim Carrey. Here she was, taking a mum of two small children to court. *Good god, give me strength,* I thought to myself, but there was nothing I could do.

Walking into the room, I found benches facing several higher sets of tables, and chairs that sat on an elevated platform, facing the bench. The applicant sat on one side, and the respondent on the other. Everything looked old and run down, and the room smelled of cleaning remedies. We all sat down, and the applicant's lawyer started talking. Fiona was seated behind Casper. She looked as if she'd found her place in life. I wished her good luck in my head, knowing I didn't mean it.

I sat there and listened to Casper's solicitor's booming voice, as I was accused of the most heinous things. I was a scorned woman who had used my kids as a weapon, poisoning their relationship with their father. I was physically abusive – I'd thrown a baby cup at his face when I'd found out about the affair. I was an alcoholic, far too unreliable to arrange anything with Casper, and essentially denied him access to his kids. I'd put dirty clothes on the children, neglected them, and starved them. On rainy days, I hadn't made sure of raincoats. The list carried on. It was suggested that perhaps the father should take sole custody of the children.

For me to mention the non-existent child support in my case was not appropriate as it was considered a financial issue and not a family law issue, in the eyes of the court. We were not allowed to bring these facts or any other financial issues relating to the kids into the court room. I wasn't allowed to question his ability to be a responsible father regarding support, nor mention that he had taken my money, and had stolen the kids' childcare money. To this day, I still try to figure out how the family residency court finds this reasonable. Surely these facts are a welfare issue? I found that it was very hard to question the court system without worrying that it would affect my credibility and my case. I was allowed to question his ability to keep our agreements regarding his visits, his ability as a father, and the issue of slander.

The court found the arrangements we'd previously made suitable, but Casper's lawyer wouldn't back down on their demands, and he started mentioning the Hague Convention, which they claimed I was in breach of, and claiming that fathers had fewer rights. The judge turned to me.

"Miss Berg, do you mind me speaking directly to you?"

What was I supposed to say?

"No, Your Honour."

My barrister tried to interrupt, saying, "Your Honour, I'm here to defend the respondent."

"I don't care who you are," the judge replied.

"But, Your Honour, Miss Berg shouldn't be directly spoken to by you."

The judge shouted, "Don't tell me what to do, Mr. Harris, or I will ask you to be quiet for the duration."

Mr. Harris looked bewildered. The judge clearly felt that he could do whatever he wanted in the courtroom, as it was his courtroom. It was perverse, but it seemed to be accepted.

The judge continued, "How do you think we can resolve this?"

I was dumbfounded – surely the man wasn't asking me the question I was paying my lawyer and barrister to answer.

"I think, if we can agree that the children need to see their father, but not as often as requested and while still living with me, then we can come to some sort of solution."

I glanced at my barrister, who was furious and biting his lip.

"I agree," the judge said.

Silence overtook the room, while the judge looked at his papers. I didn't really understand – all I wanted was to go back to my bathroom and sob into a towel. Finally, he looked up and stated that he didn't think it was fair to the father to only see the children every second weekend, and for tea once a week. I tried to explain that I was worried about the kids' environment and insisted that it would take time for them to adjust. He dismissed this, interrupting me so I couldn't finish, and explained that he saw no evidence that there was anything to be worried about. Of course, I wanted to mention the cancelled visits and the days he left them in a playground behind the pub, with only a nine-year-old to look after them, and my barrister and I were again dismissed when we tried to back my opinion up. The judge told me that my view of Casper wasn't important – it was about what was best for the kids. He wasn't listening at all, and I realised that he saw my kids as parcels that could be brought back and forth to different homes. On paper, it looked perfect, but not in reality.

I was baffled and, for a moment, thought I might faint out of pure fear. I realised that the judge wasn't going to rule on what was important for Magnus and Pepper. His ruling would be held until our next court date, which was three months away, and I had no reason to believe he'd want to listen then. He decided that the children should stay with their father every Wednesday, for an overnight stay, on top of the every second weekend we'd already agreed on. I was mortified, as I was already struggling to get the kids to go on the weekends when they weren't cancelled on.

When I walked out of the courtroom, I saw Casper and Fiona celebrating loudly. I, on the other hand, went and sat in a room with Mr. Harris, who was almost shouting at me to file a complaint about Fiona's presence, and about the judge overruling him. I had no idea what to do. I felt that if I created any hassle for anyone, I would get in trouble, and it would affect the children's lives. I didn't know my rights or how to play my cards – I just wanted to curl up and cry, but the fact was that I needed to pick up my babies, feed them, send more emails for work, and carry on. I felt like a failure, and I was sure I should have been stronger when dealing with the judge. Worst of all, I dreaded having to tell my babies that they were going to have to sleep at 'Daddy's' house one more day a week. The voices of Mr. Harris, who seemed to have had his pride stung by his performance in the courtroom, and Karen became a blur, and I resigned myself to a place in my head where I couldn't hear them. I just nodded and tried to keep calm. If I started listening, my fear would have an open door, and I would most likely collapse there and then. I wanted to keep silent and not scream, and I wanted to see my children.

I decided not to make a complaint because I couldn't see how it could go well with a judge who had already made his ruling without listening to my objections. If he wouldn't listen then, why would he change his opinion later on? I left the room and Karen gave me a hug and told me we'd nail it next time.

"In three months' time, that is," I said.

She nodded her head and smiled, as if it would encourage me. I shook Mr. Harris's hand and considered telling him that my court battle wasn't about his ego, but I was too tired.

I sat on the tube on my way home and felt as if someone had sucked all the power out of me. I was almost floating. I had no connection to my legs or my head, and the people around me seemed to be moving as if they were in a movie playing out in front of me. My thoughts shifted to my children. I believed that it was my job to make sure they didn't bump into too many sharp edges on the furniture in life. I knew that, if I moved the furniture, their opportunities would be greater and their path easier. I thought back to the courtroom and pictured the judge emptying a truckload of furniture over our heads. In this vision, my children were scared and anxious, and I had no idea how to move the furniture on my own. I looked at the people who sat in front of me and wondered if they could tell what I was going through. A guy in a suit looked at me and smirked in a flirty way, but I didn't respond. He looked back down to his phone, probably thinking that I was an uptight bitch, because that's all he saw: an uptight bitch who wanted to be in control. If only they all knew that I was just trying to do the right thing. I couldn't wait to cuddle my kids. *If the train could just go faster,* I thought.

Screaming in the Bushes

T he recession was only getting more aggressive, and more casualties were being announced every day on the news. I was now sure that closing the shop had been a smart business decision, and I found some confidence in this. It was a small victory, considering how many battles I was fighting, but a victory nonetheless.

I started an application with the CSA to try and get childcare support, but it failed, as Casper simply didn't work and had zero income, so therefore, he didn't have to pay for his kids.

In Denmark, you have the government making calculations based on how old the kids are, their needs, and the cost of living in your town or city. They pay out every month, and the father pays the government. If he doesn't, the father ends up in prison. I was increasingly worried about how the kids and I were going to survive.

I suffered through months of testing, as they measured my ability to be a mother; months of Casper's accusations. They would write vile emails at two, three, four in the morning for me to find when I switched on my computer. Casper threatened me and said he couldn't guarantee what Fiona's ex-husband, the millionaire, and his contacts would do if he found out about the toxic environment I was creating around his three sons and their little family. They would go so far sometimes as to say that when they had won the court case, I would never see my children again. It took me days to get the bad feeling under my skin to go away, and in the end, I couldn't, so I decided that at some stage, I would need therapy to help me, or Valium. I hadn't made my mind up.

We were recommended, which is the same as ordered when it comes from the court, to go through mediation as well, which I had to pay for out of my overdraft, as I was honest enough to say that I'd borrowed money from my parents. They counted this as income. Meanwhile, Casper got it for free because he had no job.

The mediation was in Twickenham, which wasn't far away from us. I took the Nissan and turned up thirty minutes early to register. I felt like I was suffocating. My anxiety had been turned up to eleven, as the pressure mounted. Casper walked in while I was in the waiting room, and he looked very polished, with a new watch, clothes, and a file under his arm. If I didn't know any better, he looked almost normal.

During mediation, we sat with a man who'd been trained to help parents understand their kids' needs. The office was on the second floor, and the room faced towards the windows. We met him first, one by one.

When I went into the office, the gentleman (who was called 'David') said, "Kat, this is not a time to be bitter – it's a time to be moving forward and forgetting what's behind you."

"I find that hard," I said, "considering he took all my money. We're now struggling to just buy food."

"As I said, you need to look forward," he said.

It hit me that he wanted us to get along as parents and, as it was everyone's wish, I nodded.

"I understand that, but it's hard trying to work it out with someone when they don't want what's best for the kids – he's taken all our money and made sure we don't have enough to eat while he walks around in Calvin Klein underwear and doesn't even see the kids on agreed dates."

"There's a lot of anger here, and we need to pass it," David said.

"Can you just be fucking real with me? If he wanted what was best for the kids, he would pay at least one hundred pounds a month towards food. He'd make sure the kids were happy and wouldn't take me to court to try to rip the kids away from their home. I mean, for fuck's sake, he cancels almost every weekend, and he doesn't help with their care in any sense. Am I going mad?"

David looked at me as if he thought I was mad. He said, "You're very angry, but we're here to move forward."

I took a deep breath.

"I'm not sure I can do this unless you acknowledge that he's the one that does nothing for his kids, and I'm the only one who is questioned about my mood."

David wrote something in his notebook. Fear gripped me, and I wondered whether I'd just delivered them another weapon. I wondered why Casper wasn't being held accountable for his actions, and why Fiona wasn't even here. I was tormented by the need to defend myself.

After Casper met David, we were put in the same room. David's first suggestion was for Casper and I to look at each other and try to find a way to communicate about the kids in an amicable way.

Casper looked at me and said, "Stop making our lives miserable, and let me get on with my life. Let the kids be a part of this."

I breathed in. Everything in me told me to take the board that was hanging neatly on the wall with 'Plan in action for us' written on it and smash it over his head. He reminded me of Dr. Jekyll and Mr. Hyde, only much worse. He had cheated the system, and our kids' welfare was at stake.

"Casper, if you could live a life with the kids and Fiona as you wish, what would it be like?"

"What do you mean?" he asked, clearly puzzled.

"I just want you to tell me how you want this to work out. Which weekends do you want?"

He was absolutely lost.

"Don't play fucking mind games with me, Kat. You know what I want."

"No, I don't, Casper. You can't even handle the weekends as they are, so why do you want more?"

"You're a liar, and you're poisoning the kids against me. You need to just start listening to me, do you hear?" I smiled; here he was, the real Casper. It wasn't about the kids, it was about me not doing what he said. He wanted to show everyone that he was the boss. He continued, "You're a failure, Kat, and you've never been happy. That's why you're doing this."

"Doing what? Affairs, taking you to court, writing vile emails that threaten me? I'm confused; doing *what*, Casper?"

"This is all your fault," he spat, twitching in his chair. "If you could just listen and do what I say, you wouldn't have any problems. It would never have come to this!"

I glanced at David. What if he thought this was okay? Why wasn't he telling Casper not to be angry and to move forward? I turned back to Casper.

"Go fuck yourself, Casper. You're a sad piece of shit. You've never thought about the kids – if you had, you wouldn't have taken their money, you would see them when you promise, you would read bedtime stories to them, you would care about them asking for their mummy when you keep them for days without my agreement, you wouldn't use them as a tool to try to make a point. But here we are, me paying for mediation to ask you to do the right thing by your kids, so fuck you, Casper, and you too,

David, for making me feel like I'm the one who's wrong. Shame on you both for allowing me to feel this way. You have failed in fatherhood, Casper. Again, answer me: why are you dragging me through this? Why are you dragging the kids through this?"

"I think I might be missing some information about your past," said David, looking lost. "Can you explain to me again the alleged incident where the kids stayed away for longer than agreed?"

Casper looked at David, and I could see he was about to lose it. I was tearing up and I took my jacket and handbag and turned to David. "Where do I need to pay for this session?"

"By the way, your language is unacceptable, but if you must go, you need to write a cheque to me at reception."

I nodded.

"Well, David, if it's not amicable, it often isn't pretty, so maybe next time, take a stand for the kids, and get real with what's happening around you. I'll leave the cheque downstairs."

Casper sat in his chair, smirking but red-faced. I couldn't give a fuck; I was furious. I walked out, breathed the fresh air through the rain, and walked towards my old Nissan, hoping it would start. I knew the fear would come back, but right now, I felt good. I'd stood up for myself and for the kids. I would call Karen later and tell her what a disappointment the session had been, but right now, I felt amazing, even with the tears streaming down my cheeks.

I sobbed all the way home. The fear kicked in quicker than I'd anticipated, and the feeling of victory faded fast. I started doubting if it was even worth living with this fear – it was the first time I'd considered giving in to their demands. *Please, fear, give me a moment to breathe, please.*

The three months were long, and I still struggled to get Casper to keep to his weekends. When I asked him to take the kids to a birthday party on his weekend, he would refuse, saying it wasn't up to me to organise his weekends. When he finally collected the kids, his weekends were isolated from the kids' social lives, and it almost seemed as if they'd disappeared from the surface of the Earth. I found it unhealthy, but I was, by law, not allowed to obstruct him.

The court and solicitors had given me no warning as to how tough this was going to be. It was around this time that my panic attacks were uncontrollable. I would lie down at night and simply not be able to breathe. It was like an elephant was sitting on my chest. I'd be nearly falling asleep, listening to Rosie's breathing, and my thoughts would wander. How was I going to pay the bills? What new abuse would I receive from Casper and his crew? How could I get on top of all the business stuff? How would my kids cope with everything that was going on? Then, all at once, I would have this tickling feeling in my legs and my arms, and I would feel that I couldn't catch my breath. It felt like someone had taken the oxygen out of my bedroom. I would sit up, put the lights on, and look at Rosie snoring away. My brain would tell me that if she could breathe, I should be able to, too. I would cling to my bed frame, feeling as if I was dying, and then I would get angry about the fact that my kids had to go live with their stupid father. This anger actually sometimes made me snap out of the panic attacks more quickly, after which I would sob quietly, and then fall asleep after a few hours. I'd be even more exhausted the next day and, as my anxiety attacks could be triggered by tiredness, they quickly became something I had to learn to live with on an everyday basis.

Kirsten told me that after her ordeals with her ex-husband, she began screaming on her dog walks with Sonny. She told me it was a good way to release endorphins and was a great stress reliever. I was hesitant to follow in her footsteps, but I was also in need of a resolution. I remembered the day in the shop and how good I had felt after. I had bags under my eyes so dark that even Polyfilla wouldn't help, and I was fragile and vulnerable. It was coming to a point where I was becoming paranoid – I almost felt that people were looking at me and thinking I was a terrible person. *A terrible mother.*

One day, while walking Rosie in the park, I decided to try screaming. I looked to my right and to my left, breathed in, and screamed. I felt terribly silly. I tried on my next attempt to scream at a higher note, but I sounded like I was speaking to the green parrots flying around me. I walked home texting Kirsten, telling her that I didn't feel liberated in any way, and instead just felt stupid. She texted back saying, 'You're not doing it right, Kat. You've really got to scream, like nothing else matters.'

I went out the next day and screamed so loud that I became dizzy for a moment and felt a slight headache coming on. Rosie looked up at me as if I was mad. I screamed more into the bushes and suddenly felt the emptiness – the sheer peace of thoughtlessness and fearlessness. I looked up into the sky and felt light, and at peace, for the first time in a long time. Some people walked past and looked at me funny, but it seemed like a small price to pay. It felt good, and I needed that, because it was all I could do.

Over the three months, things escalated. I had to figure out how to keep the bailiffs away. One set of bailiffs had rung the doorbell, and two large men had claimed that I hadn't paid a supplier at a flower wholesale market. I asked them for more details, and it turned out that Casper had started his own project and had set up a new flower shop with Fiona. He had bought flowers in my company name. I was livid and told them both to fuck off before I called the police.

The day after, I locked myself in the toilet, after the kids had gone to bed, tied towels around my wrists, tied the towels to the towel hanger, and stuck a flannel in my mouth. I screamed my lungs out while pulling against the towels. I was in there for more than ten minutes, which is a long time to sit and scream. I screamed out every ounce of fear, anger, and frustration. I didn't know where else to put all these emotions – I had to protect my kids from my insecurities, as they had enough instability to deal

with. I couldn't confront Casper, as this would give him ammuni-
tion regarding my hostile behaviour. I couldn't use it in court, and
my friends were getting tired of me moaning all the time.
Camilla, Steve, Sam, and Paul had been non-existent over the
preceding months. I had called Camilla one night and asked her if
she could come around, as I was feeling fragile.

"Can we share a frozen pizza and a cheap bottle of wine?"

"I can't, my love; I've promised to make a lasagne for the
neighbour. She's just had an extension built, and she's going
through so much with no kitchen. I'll call you tomorrow."

She never did. Meanwhile, Polly and Kirsten needed a break if
I was going to keep them as friends. *Just breathe Kat, breathe.*

I had to be strong for clients and be enthusiastic about their
weddings and events. I genuinely cared for all my clients, but let's
be honest, it's no fun sitting there and listening to someone talk
about how in love and happy they are, especially when they
clearly have so much money to spend. Meanwhile, I couldn't even
pay for food. I felt terrible for having these thoughts and feelings
but, if I could, I would have told them all to take their money and
run off. I just wanted to focus on my kids. I nurtured the fact that
this would probably be the scariest thing in my life. Often,
between client meetings, I had to go to the ladies' room and just
sit on the floor, doing breathing exercises or wiping my eyes. I
became a frequent user of eye drops, either due to lack of sleep or
from crying my eyes out all the time. Sometimes, during client
meetings, my BlackBerry would be beeping with emails as I
received my daily abuse from Fiona, telling me what an awful
mum I was and how full of anger I was. Fiona couldn't seem to
get over my apparent jealousy and resentment of their newfound
love and family unit. There was no point in telling her what
Casper had done because she believed everything he said. I
wondered why she didn't spend more time caring for her own
children, who had also just experienced parental separation. She
was obsessed with me, it seemed, and Casper had given her the

green light to say and act in any way she wanted. This made sense, as she was his meal ticket. It was a chaotic time, but I also wondered how a mother could do this to another mother.

Kirsten told me to turn off email notifications on my phone.

"Leave the emails to your laptop or computer or whatever device you have that Casper hasn't taken. Just switch it off – the emails will be there when you go into your office and, believe me, it will do you a world of good."

Pippi Longstocking

Three months had gone by, and we were back in court.
Kirsten drove me this time, and I was greeted by Mr.
Harris and Karen. I had arranged to go home with her, and I
would be picked up at the station in Richmond. Same building,
same procedure, same process, same anxiety and trembling.
Karen explained that they would go for the case that the judge
hadn't listened last time, and also warned me that each time, it
could be a different judge. We got called into the court room, and
it *was* a different judge. This time, Fiona wasn't there, and Casper
looked much more vulnerable.

Arguing that the children seemed more restless and that
Casper had cancelled quite a lot of the Wednesday night sleep-
overs, the judge ordered the weekday gone, and also that the
Children and Family Court Advisory and Support Service (or
'CafCass') be involved. Due to the children's welfare being questioned by Casper and myself, the court ordered an investigation,
and a report from them to decide if there was any truth in the
allegations. It was apparently normal practice, and the judge gave
the new hearing date as six months away, along with the new
parameters for visitation.

I walked a little lighter, mentally and physically, for the first time, and I hugged Karen and Mr. Harris. Afterwards, I went to the train station. I texted Kirsten that I would be there soon, but there was no need to collect me, as I had good news.

CafCass took care to contact everyone involved, including the nursery, both sides' parents, and Fiona and her sons. This aggravated Fiona, as she blamed me for her life being scrutinised. It was a joke. When the social worker visited Casper, he wasn't even home. Instead, Fiona met them with the children and the family social worker. It showed me that he had finally given up on trying to lie to the rest of the world, but Fiona believed what he had told her. He didn't show up until an hour later, but by this point, Fiona would have spent some time playing the fairy godmother. It gave me great relief, because it seemed that this was how it needed to happen in order for the court system to start taking me seriously as a mother, and not as the 'scorned woman'.

It was my turn next, and the social worker came to my house and rang the doorbell. I'd been cleaning for hours and felt sick. Here was a woman with the power to tell the court if I was a good mum or not. Nevertheless, I'd cut watermelon and arranged it beautifully on a tray on the table. The house was looking spectacular. I opened the door and she came in, sat down, and started talking immediately.

"Hi, my name is Kathy, and today we're just going to act like it's a normal day. I'll ask your children a few questions."

I looked at her, with her Pippi Longstocking plaits, her hippie skirt, her home-knitted jumper, and her square-shaped shoes, thinking, *Do you think we have social workers in our house on an everyday basis?*

"Okay," I replied, "let's be normal." The kids were looking at her as if she was Mary Poppins, and I was hoping that she would pull her umbrella out and fly out of the window sooner rather than later.

First, she asked the twins to draw a picture of Mummy's house and one of Daddy's house. Mummy's house had a large sun, large windows, and lots of happy colours. Daddy's house was big, but the windows were very small, and the sky was grey, with dark clouds. When they'd finished, Kathy took the drawings and told the kids to go and have some watermelon. The kids started to eat from the tray, and were ever so excited about having Mary Poppins in our house. Looking at the picture they'd drawn of my house made me smile. I understood what Kathy was trying to do.

Then, suddenly, Magnus came running in with a huge knife I'd used to cut the watermelon. I'd totally forgotten to take it away from the table, and my whole face dropped in horror.

"Magnus!" I shouted, full of fear.

He froze and dropped the knife, inches away from his bare toes. I was mortified. I ran to Magnus and cuddled him, and Kathy laughed and took the knife away.

"I think we better put this in a safe place."

I fell down on the couch and admitted to myself that the picture I'd been trying to paint had just been screwed up and thrown in the bin. I'd cleaned every corner of the house, removed every sharp item, and made it the Betty Crocker household, knowing that it probably wasn't important. Now, I wished I hadn't tried so hard.

She asked me and the children a few more questions and then took the drawings and wrote some notes. I was assured I'd hear from her shortly, and warned not to forget about my coming interview. She left with no indication of how the two hours had gone. It's an odd feeling to let some stranger play with your kids while also knowing that their opinion could have a huge effect on the outcome of the court's decision. The knife incident played in my mind for days. If I'd just been able to unplug my brain for a few hours, I could have regained my strength. Weeks went by, and my worries were directed towards new battles. I knew that the kids had been affected, and I felt that I was failing, as a mum and as a protector.

Then it was my time to be interviewed. The offices were in Kingston. I remember walking into this small room and sitting opposite Kathy. She had the same plaits, and still looked like Pippi. As a child, I always watched Pippi Longstocking on the telly. I remembered how she could lift her horse in the air, her friends Annika and Tommy, and her famous line when Tommy asked, "Who is the strongest man in the world?" She would always reply, "But I am the strongest girl in the world, don't forget that." *I wanted to be Pippi, just for a moment.*

Kathy was wearing multi-coloured woollen socks and looked like a true hippie. A file was on the table, and I guessed it was mine. How the kids and I ended up in a file is still a wonder to me. I didn't get a glass of water or anything, and she started asking me questions almost straightaway.

"Do you drink too much?"

I answered 'yes', as I did drink wine every day after work – after all, I was under a huge amount of stress. I didn't want to take sleeping tablets, in case there was a fire. The thought that my kids would have to rescue themselves and see Mummy burn to ashes in a flaming house kept me away.

She asked me if I had ever been physically violent. Again, I answered 'yes', as I had hit Casper with a plastic baby cup when I'd found out he'd cheated again. It had felt good. I'd also thrown his phone in the bath when I'd realised he was still in contact with Fiona while living under my roof.

The questioning went on for three hours. Kathy asked me about everything, from why I hadn't given Casper raincoats for the kids on a rainy day to why I didn't answer his call at nine in the evening on a certain date. I explained that his attempts to contact me were hostile – I could, I said, show her records of messages and calls on both my home phone and my mobile. She finished off by asking me if I had anything to add. I gave her a list of all the weekend dates Casper had cancelled over the past three months. He'd cancelled on almost seventy percent of the scheduled dates. The weekly overnight sleeps had only materialised once. She finished by writing lots of notes in silence. I looked at the room. There was hardly any furniture – two chairs and a bookshelf with trays of paper. The walls were blue, and the room was quite gloomy. It was a room with many purposes – not Kathy's office, I kept thinking, and guessing what other kinds of consultation it was used for. My mind was all over the place, and it seemed it was in survival mode, making my concentration go to other places as she wrote notes about my kids' future. She told me she would interview Casper as well, and she would give her report to the courts in due time.

"Goodbye, Kat. I hope the twins are well, and it was nice meeting you."

"You too, Kathy." I looked at her and had no idea what to say.

I said my goodbyes and left. I was exhausted and trembling. I went outside and threw up behind my car, then went to the nursery to collect the twins and play happy Mum. I couldn't believe that their father, their flesh and blood, really thought that they'd be better off without their mum. I knew I was the target, and he was happy to use his kids to get to me. He was close – I could feel my body slowly breaking, my mind slipping into a very dark place of numbness, and the lioness wanting to go to sleep in a corner, already wounded. If the court had allowed me to show them everything, they'd have had a better view of who this man was, and I would have had less fear and anxiety, and could ultimately function better as a mum. All I'd done was throw him out after his many affairs and stopped him from using my money. Now, he wanted to take away the most precious things I had. I was astonished that a mother of three had joined with Casper and shared his way of thinking. Could they really convince everyone that I was a bad mother? Would the system believe their lies? Doubt began to creep into my mind again.

The next day, I had to go to a meeting with a client to sell them on my wedding skills. Beforehand, I went to my office in the lounge and replied to emails. An unpaid tax bill told me I owed British Gas £800. Being at the mercy of other people was killing my spirit. They talked down to me, threatened me, bullied me, and kept me hanging on a thin rope, knowing they could cut the ties at any moment and plunge me into more trouble. There would be more fees, and I would be less able to defend myself. The more you owe, the less help there is. On top of this, I had to deal with some guy with small-man syndrome on the other end of the phone, saying, "Miss Berg, we have the power to switch your gas and electrics off," or, "Miss Berg, we can send a bailiff, and we can still take full payment."

It goes without saying that, on that day, I used all my eye drops. I even completed my screaming exercise in the bathroom again that same evening, after dealing with my debts. When you're mentally beaten and physically exhausted, no logical thought goes through you. It's all based on fear. The presence of money, or the lack of it, has profound physical, mental, and emotional repercussions. Some of my friends didn't understand what I was going through; all I wanted them to do was just listen when I sobbed down the phone about my problems. I already knew they couldn't fix anything, but they could listen. I lost some of my oldest friends during this period, as they simply couldn't empathise.

Dealing with this sort of stuff is powerful. For some of my friends, it was simply irritating. They stopped asking how I was or inviting me to gatherings. Every time I did show up, I couldn't be my dazzling, funny self. I would be whimpering after two glasses of wine and not have much to tell, apart from drama around the kids' residence battle. On the other hand, their problems with husbands and work seemed more 'normal', and they quickly left me to it. Visits were very rare, and it was just the kids' birthdays I got invited to.

Daniel, who I had lived with in Fulham, above the pub, had been less present, as he had met a girl. He deserved it, but he was more distant than ever. He was the kids' godfather, and had hardly seen them, as of late. I created their flowers in return for money I had borrowed from him, and the wedding was beautiful. At the venue where they got married, there were cute messages for all the guests placed on their plates. Mine said, 'Divorced Americans are the most unhappy people in the world, with the possible exception of married Scandinavians, bye bye love 1995.' I was mortified. It would have been funny if I hadn't been dealing with all the shit I was going through.

Camilla got married to Steve at a registry office. She phoned me to say that she had asked Sam and Paul for the witness part, as there were two of them and it was more practical, despite us having a friendship of twenty years, she needed me to be with someone in order to be part of it. They had gone to the pub after, just fifteen minutes away from my house, had celebrated with prosecco and with the kids playing around their feet, and they hadn't called as I 'had so much on', they thought. It was evident I wasn't fitting in, anymore. *It's so unkind of you; I need you now more than ever,* was my only thought.

I carried on working, to the point that I lost the ability to sleep. I was waiting for the report from Kathy that would decide my kids' future. Finally, it arrived, eight weeks later. Based on CafCass's recommendations and the report, Casper was to have limited contact, and their advice to the court was to give me full custody, or what they called 'residence'. The decision had been based on Casper's inability to understand the children's needs, and his obsession with controlling me and the situation. For some reason, I still had some tiny hope that I'd find something in the report that indicated that Casper loved his children more than himself, but there was nothing. Casper's version of events was that we had started a business together, I'd become an alcoholic, I'd gotten physically violent, and that I'd suffered from postnatal depression. Apparently, my parents were drunken tyrants who had ruined his life and our relationship. He also claimed he'd given me the house he'd paid the mortgage for, and had given me his fifty percent of the business. On paper, he sounded like the victim.

The report was both sad and relieving at the same time. I was so sad for my kids, but I was happy that they were going to stay with me, if the judge agreed.

My solicitor Karen called me.

"Kat, have you received the report?" I told her I had. "It could not be any better than this. Kat, aren't you happy?"

I wasn't sure what to answer.

The six months were up, and we went back to court. Again, Casper turned up on his own. In court, he tried to slander me but, as he was now representing himself, he had no one to keep him on a straight line. No lawyer was present. The judge was different again. Same building, same procedure, but less anxiety for me. I was told by my solicitor to not be so trashy in my language and to be dignified. It was difficult when I had been told for so long to be quiet. Let's be honest: I almost lost it several times. One of my fantasies was just to get him naked in an open field and throw shit at him. It seemed fair, after the hurt he had caused me and our kids.

I was dealing with a couple who thought they didn't need any advice from legal experts or any system. I think this made Casper feel like a success – he could pretend he was too knowledgeable to ask a lawyer. After all, he had Fiona to help him, sitting together as they wrote and prepared court files and statements. He felt powerful, and she was just a fool, exorcising her own demons against me. Fiona's absence surprised me but, as my solicitor said, it would have looked even worse for her to show up with a smirk on her face after CafCass's report.

The judge encouraged us to continue with mediation, but it was merely to set a final court date and make sure all parties involved had all the information and were prepared for the final hearing. A final decision on the children's future would be made shortly after, at a different date. Casper and I couldn't even speak to each other at this point. He struggled to explain why he had demanded shared care in the first place, and the judge ordered us to go on a parents' course. He was unwilling to do so, but I agreed. I had nothing to lose and everything to gain. His success quickly crumbled in front of me, and it seemed that it had been Fiona's work, and he actually had no idea what he was trying to represent.

I walked away from the building that day feeling light and positive for the first time in a very long time. The upheaval of my children's lives seemed to have been averted. They would still see their father, but in an organised and (hopefully) conflict-free manner. They would slowly get used to the major changes. I felt that the bag that had been dragged over their heads, just so they could fit into their father's new life, had now been taken off. They could breathe freely, at last, and take things slow. Now, I just needed the residence order to be mine, so I didn't have to live in fear of Casper's next stunt.

Fiona kept emailing me and, when I asked why, she said, "He wasn't as fortunate as me in his education, and was not brought up in the same way as you, Katja. Therefore, I am helping him in this very difficult time." *She's one of a kind,* I thought.

During the mediation, we tried endlessly to figure out the visitations. Casper continued to cancel and change weekends, and the trial went on unnecessarily, as he still believed he could win. I decided to accept an offer from my parents to go to Denmark with the children for a summer holiday. As we were in a legal battle, I had to get permission from Casper before I took the children out of the country. Casper agreed via email, as he had already sorted his own holidays out. My parents paid for cheap tickets, as I had no money.

Casper texted me one night and asked me if I was considering staying in Denmark and not to forget that they had already filed their concerns regarding the Hague Convention. This was a law that had been created to keep children in the country they were born in, and not to travel without both parents' approval. I wrote back that the kids had a full life in England, and I had a mortgage and a business to get back to. He decided that I wasn't being honest with him, and I dismissed the texts as drunken ramblings and let it be.

In the following days, Casper accused me of planning to kidnap the children and move them to Denmark, ignoring the fact that I had an email where he'd agreed to the trip. He actually forced me to go to court, and it ended up costing me another £1200 in lawyers' fees. I had to sign an agreement in front of the judge saying that, if I didn't bring the children back on a certain date for him to collect at the airport, I could face jail. The beauty of the court system meant that he didn't have to show up himself in court – he only had to make the accusation.

The cost of the application meant that the kids and I had even less money to live on. We finally went away and I again just slept, ate, and gathered my strength while my parents saw their beloved grandchildren.

When we came back, Casper cancelled on collecting the children at the airport, as the court had ordered, because he and Fiona had decided to go to Spain that weekend. I scrambled our bags together, and we went to the train station, me and two disappointed kids sitting on a hot tube. They wanted to see their dad.

We had reached the final court hearing – our last chance to rip each other's skin off, and then the final decision would be made a few days after. Sixteen months had gone by. I was nervous, but Casper had messed up so many times, so it didn't look good for him. I still had anxiety because I'd had so many disappointments thus far.

This time, the court was in a different building. It was bigger, and felt like one of the courtrooms you see in movies. The adrenaline began to kick in as I waited for the session to begin. The fear grabbed me again, but I wasn't sure how to fight it anymore. My barrister Mr. Harris and I sat down, with Karen behind us, and Casper walked in all on his own. No lawyers, no Fiona; just him. He was carrying a big file under his arm, which I knew for sure he hadn't organised himself. He wouldn't be able to find his own asshole if you gave him a map.

We were called in and sat on benches, while we waited for the honourable judge. The judge walked in, and I saw it was a different judge again. Casper gave his case, fumbling and mumbling through it all. Mr. Harris had a hard time keeping his smile back, to the extent that he had to bite his lip. It was then our turn to defend, and Mr. Harris gave a full report of the last sixteen months' events, which was already filed. Court was adjourned for a break, and we went to a Pret A Manger to have a sandwich, although I couldn't eat. Walking back to the building, I was numb. I couldn't speak, I couldn't think; I just wanted the final decision.

We all sat in the same places and had to stand up when the judge walked in. He sat down, and we all sat down. He took a breath and began to speak.

"Mr. Casper Stein, it is clear to me that you have not honoured your own children's needs. You have not kept to prearranged visitations, you have not followed the court's guidance, and you have, above all, behaved in the most inappropriate manner towards everyone involved in this case. You have a profoundly wrongful view of what is best for your children, and I can tell you now that no judge will give you any residency rights, in this case. I think you are lucky if the mother, the respondent, will allow you any visitation rights at all. I am not confident that you are committed to the children's safety and care. It seems to me that you have created most of the crossfires here, and have not lent any support, nor any thought, to what is best for Magnus and Pepper. It is with regret that I see how far the respondent has been dragged through this, and I will honour the CafCass report as a final evidence in giving her the full residence order. That is what the final court decision should be. This will be my final response."

Casper tried, "Your Honour—"

The judge slammed his gavel down and almost shouted, "Mr. Stein, the only thing I will hear from you in this court are remorseful words. You have wasted everyone's time, and you have created a situation where there are not only two victims – your children – but three, for I must include their mother. You should be ashamed of yourself." The judge looked at me. "I am sorry, Miss Berg, for the toll that this trial has taken on you."

Afterwards, I stood there as a feeling of peace washed over my body, like a warm blanket had been placed over my shoulders. I started to feel tired and suddenly tearful, but no tears came. Karen was hugging me, and my barrister asked me to step outside. Casper ran out of the courtroom, dialling his phone. Mr. Harris asked me quickly if I would allow him to speak to Casper and offer him a full financial settlement, on our behalf, if he agreed to sign me over full custody now, instead of after the final round in a few days' time. I looked at Karen, who nodded, and my barrister ran after Casper. He came back twenty minutes later and told me that Casper had agreed, so long as I paid his settlement fees. He'd given up custody there and then.

I walked outside, and the air hit me with a feeling of freedom I hadn't felt in months. I closed my eyes. I couldn't wait to see my babies, kiss them, hug them, smell them, all while knowing they were staying with me, and that we could finally continue our lives. I opened my eyes to find Fiona standing there, on her own, looking at me. She was dressed all in black, and her face looked like a bulldog chewing a wasp. I smiled and walked away with Mr. Harris and Karen to find a café where we could sort all the papers out. I called my parents and my father cried down the phone as he said, "Oh my god, it's finally over! The kids are safe."

I paid for the handling of the case and for the legal papers, which would state I had full residency. There was no contact agreement put in place, and Casper didn't ask for one. One week later, the papers were signed, and I had a new bill of £3000 to deal with, which I paid in instalments. Soon, everything went quiet – there were no emails or texts, and Casper said he was going away with Fiona and her kids for six weeks, to heal the wounds. I wondered how they would explain themselves, now. He still didn't ask for any visitation rights and, when I offered, he ignored me.

I wondered why Fiona and I, as women, mothers, and members of the sisterhood, had fought. Why did she get so involved? She didn't know who I was, or what I stood for, or what I had been through. Why didn't she let me and Casper just fight it out? But it's like they say: 'Holding a grudge is like drinking poison and waiting for the other person to die.'

Single Mother Strikes Back

It took a few months before anything started to settle. I started therapy because I didn't know where to put the anger, hate, and tears. The kids would get upset when they saw me cry, and I'd sometimes catch myself planning my revenge on Fiona and Casper. They'd taken my livelihood and nearly the entire last two years of my life, after all, and they had upset my children. I wanted to stop and focus, instead, on the future.

Casper was still angry about not getting his way. He started a rumour that he had left me the house and the money, and had been a victim of the 'fathers have no rights' trend. Meanwhile, he didn't see the twins or even suggest doing so. He spent his days blabbing on at pubs or dinner parties. I stopped trying to rationalise his behaviour, as it was the only way I could manage him. What struck me was that a lot of people seemed to believe him. His family was sure he was telling the truth, even though they knew him well. His sister was the only one who really seemed to see him for what he was. Some of our shared friends were reluctant to take sides, and I became resentful. There was wrong and there was right, and he was clearly in the wrong. As a result, I lost even more friends.

Even after many months at the therapist's office, I was still working to become a better person. I wanted to make better choices and avoid being fooled by men like Casper. If you know better, you do better. I invested in myself emotionally. 'No more bullshit from anyone,' was my new motto. Life was too short. I learned that not staying true to yourself was the same as lying to all your friends and family.

I do know, from my experiences in court, that the legal system is flawed in many ways. Why, for example, was Casper able to run off with all my money? My bank manager and I spent hours amassing evidence, proving how Casper had emptied my accounts, but no one gave a shit.

After Casper lost in court, his and Fiona's relationship began to fizzle out. The business they had started together had closed down, and he had met another woman on an online dating site. Rumour has it that he took over £70,000 from Fiona. The day I heard that, I was the one smirking in silence. His new love was a Brazilian woman named 'Carolina' and, to be honest, I thought she was crazy and obsessive, but overall, I liked her. She had dark hair, was curvy in a sexy way, and was flamboyant in her behaviour. She always asked about the kids – it was like having a normal conversation with someone who understood what it was like to be part of a split family. Casper, of course, moved quickly into her home and, as the kids had finally gotten used to being in a split family, I didn't mind when she was introduced to the children. I accepted the fact that I couldn't be responsible for Casper's actions as a father. I could only make sure my children were safe and well-looked after.

Still, he did continue to mess up. While he was with Carolina, he began planning to move to Holland, without telling her. I continued trying to get him to pay his share of the debts, but he kept running away. I had no legal power over him, as we weren't married, which turned out to be a good thing, or he could have taken half the house. He soon went into voluntary bankruptcy, leaving me with debts of over £100,000. I had escaped his claws, but now I was in the claws of eight different companies and banks. On top of this, I owed friends over £8000 in personal loans.

At this time, I was still eight stone, not sleeping, and was having panic attacks over how I was going to pay the next bill. I soon realised that throwing myself into a new relationship might be a form of escapism; maybe someone could even rescue me. However, I would have left the relationship as soon as I'd felt better, which wouldn't have been fair. On top of this, I knew that your children are only yours for a short while, and it was important to me to make sure they could one day look back on their lives and know that they were loved, and that they'd been raised right. For them, I had to soldier on. The lioness was slowly recovering.

Ploughing through a day of meetings with clients, while simultaneously trying to generate money and discovering more debts, became normal to me. One day, I discovered a Casper stunt that managed to shock me, even after everything else he'd done. I received a letter from the nursery informing me that I was in arrears, which was normal for me, but the amount had tripled. I went to talk to Emma, the manager, who looked at me, clearly quite uncomfortable. She explained that I only had a week to pay up, as head office weren't happy that I had increased the debt, instead of paying it off. Seeing the accounts, I realised that he had emptied the kids' nursery account again, spent the money, and not told me – but then again, why would he? As a parent, he had a right to access the account and I needed a costly court decision to remove him, so I had opted not to. I apologised to her and said there must be a mistake, and that I would make sure payment was made within the week. I went and grabbed the kids, and my autopilot kicked in – I said all the right things to passing mums, put the kids in the car, and drove home, my face beetroot-coloured. At home, I found that Casper had transferred all the money to his personal account. He hadn't even tried to hide it. I mean, just how cold could this fucker get?

I sat on the kitchen floor sobbing, not knowing how to deal with yet more debt. The phone rang, and I saw it was Kirsten.

She asked, "Kat, are you okay?"

I tried to sound normal, saying I would call her later.

"I think I know what's going on. How much do you need?" she asked. I told her about what Casper had done.

"I'll see you in an hour," she said. "Don't do anything stupid."

I must have sounded terrible for her to say something like that. She rang the doorbell an hour later, and was laden with Sainsbury's bags full of shopping. She marched in and filled up my fridge and freezer.

She sat me down, handed me an envelope and said, "Here's the money to clear your debt with the nursery. We don't want the money back, we just want you back on your feet. Aiden says hi."

Of course, I started crying. I couldn't control myself. It was one of the kindest things anyone had ever done for me. She cooked us up a meal and left, reassured that I was in a better place. After tucking the kids into bed, I crawled into my own bed. I was grateful for having such people around me. I was grateful for my children, who were safe with me. I was grateful that I hadn't yet had a nervous breakdown. All that being said, I was very fucking pissed off with the universe for putting me through all this shit.

The next day, I contacted Casper. He denied knowing it was for the nursery, but stated that he'd left me the house, even though he knew he'd never paid for it. He told me my financial problems were my own fault, and that he had ended up with nothing. I put the phone down, thinking I could either cry snot bubbles or just carry on.

I kept working and found some potential solutions that might improve my situation. Someone told me I was probably eligible for a work tax credit, and maybe some discount on the council tax, so I phoned the council and told them I was in a really bad state, financially. They told me that, if I sold the house, I'd be able to pay off most of the debts, and I, of course, acknowledged that. Having a company gave me the flexibility to take care of the kids, which meant I could save on childcare, but if I went into a nine-to-five job, I'd have to pay for childcare. It was making my head spin.

I was told by the council that they'd registered my name, in case I lost my house, but that I wouldn't get any help, otherwise.

I remember exactly what the guy said, "We don't help people who have a pot of gold."

I asked, "What do you mean?"

"You have a house, don't you?"

"Yes, but I'll have to sell it, as I can't afford the debts, bills, and mortgage. I simply have no money for me and the kids to eat."

"Well, the people we help have never had that luxury, so I suggest you find someone else to help with your problems."

I suppose he was right, but I'm not so sure that having a house should automatically mean that a person doesn't deserve help. I had paid over £90,000 in taxes, and I wasn't looking to sit at home moaning – I wanted to get debt-free and work. I just needed a little help to get started, but the same system that allowed Casper to go bankrupt stopped me from looking after my kids. Again, there was the feeling of obscurity in the system. 'Bollocks' is the only word that came to mind, and I said it over and over again, until the man on the other end of the phone hung up.

I took my engagement ring and walked to Richmond high street, intent on finding the jeweller who would give me the most money for it. What broke my heart was that the stones symbolised Magnus and Pepper. I was well aware that it was me who'd paid for the ring, in the first place. I knew that leaving Casper had been the right thing to do, but it didn't mean that I was happy the kids would never have a present father in their lives. In the end, I got £250 for the ring, no questions asked. I thanked the lady behind the till and went to do some food shopping, my five-pounds-a-day budget system at the ready.

I had loads of meetings with the Citizens Advice Bureau and one with a lawyer, who confirmed that, if I went bankrupt, the debt collectors would still come after me. After all, I still had an asset – the house – but thanks to the recession and its aftermath, there was no equity in it, so selling it would actually have left me with more debt. I stopped chasing the council. I was trapped, and I'd spend each day shovelling around piles of envelopes from debt collectors.

The pressure was out of this world, and it slowly ate me up, until there was barely anything left. I'd cry at the smallest things, and no one understood why I was so fragile, because they didn't feel it every day. It became normal, and I wouldn't wish it on anyone. What was almost worse was how people would scrutinise me. Some of my oldest friends began to think that I was a pain to be with and couldn't understand why I couldn't just pull it together. When they went out to a restaurant, I would say, "We've already eaten," as I knew my card would bounce.

I remember Sam calling me. I hadn't been able to get hold of her for a while, and I assumed she wasn't interested in the same shit I had to tell her, every time.

"Hi, how are you?" I said.

"I'm good, and you?" After lots of chit chat, she announced, "We just booked a villa with Camilla and Steve to go to Italy, this summer!" I was silent for a while, and it hit her. "Oh, did you want to come? We thought you didn't have any money, or that you'd be working, but I'm sure we can figure something out."

"You're right, I have no money, but it would have been nice to have been asked, as a part of our group."

"Oh, I'm so sorry. It just seemed easier with the logistics and—"

I had no clue what she meant, but it was obvious I didn't fit in.

"It's okay. As you said, I couldn't afford it, anyway."

I made my excuses, put the phone down, and cried. I was broken, and now my closest friends couldn't even be bothered to include me in their plans. *How lonely can you get?* I pulled away from these people – I'd had enough. We women are strong, but we should remember to treat each other with kindness. Don't judge, for Christ's sake: it's so not okay, women.

So, I drank more red wine, cried, lost even more weight, and became more paranoid about how people thought I was doing. One morning, I broke down in front of my son, and all the other parents, during morning rush, when he shouted, "Don't go, Mummy! Don't go, Mummy!"

Not one mother asked me if I was alright. They walked past me quickly. Maybe, at their kindest, they found it sad, but no one asked me if I was okay. Judging someone doesn't define the person you judge, but it defines you. So listen up, ladies – when you see a mum crying with her kid, maybe ask if there's something you can do to help, instead of looking down on her. If she doesn't want your help, she'll tell you, but she'll know that you cared, and she'll feel less alone.

I calmed my son down and told him that Mummy had happy tears in her eyes, and that she would come back. It broke my heart, as all I wanted to do was scoop my kids up, lie on our couch with lots of duvets, and watch family cartoons. Instead, I left them at nursery, had another cry in my shitty Nissan, and went to a meeting.

A few days later, I went to the doctor to try to get some therapeutic help on the NHS. My own therapist, Petra, was helpful, but I'd run out of money. I was offered Prozac, but declined, as I was sure it wasn't a chemical problem, but was instead related to my emotional coping skills.

The doctor said, "I know, it's only because it'll be six months before you can get some therapy on the NHS, so I thought it would be good, until then."

I declined again and borrowed some more money from my parents, as they were growing more concerned about my health.

Back at my private therapist's office, I cried for an hour. It was forty-five pounds spent on something I was constantly doing on my own, anyway. My therapist was in her late fifties, looked kind, and was a good listener, but her office was tiny and felt quite claustrophobic. I remember how, as soon as she said that my life wasn't normal, I just cried. For someone on the outside, who didn't know me, to tell me that what I was going through wasn't normal, was momentous, especially when some of my closest friends couldn't support me. All I could do was cry snot bobbles over and over again, and I remember just shaking and trying to stammer my worries out to her.

After a few visits, it got better. I learned to fight back mentally, to look after myself and the children, and to be confident. Being confident when, for so long, I'd been embattled was a real shot in the arm. For the first time in a long while, I straightened my back, lifted my head, and saw what was truly around me. I knew I had to live by the principle that, as long as I was true to myself and did the right thing, I wouldn't have to worry. Ultimately, I got to know myself, for better or for worse.

It was hard work, and it was scary to go so deep within myself, but now I was the real me. I wasn't scared, and I understood that even when you owe people money, it doesn't mean they can tell you who you are or what to spend the money on. Friends and family who have helped you can have an opinion about your situation, but that doesn't mean they're allowed to shove it down your throat. People who do this aren't kind, and they need to be filtered out of your life.

I kept going to see my therapist and, piece by piece, I organised my emotions into boxes. I learned to separate what's important from what isn't. Through this process, I'm now able to

understand my panic attacks and why I get them, and I'm therefore better able to avoid them. I now understand that being sad is
okay – people who don't think so can move along with their day,
and I will walk in the opposite direction.

I still worked from five in the morning onwards. I had to get
on top of debt collectors and work, and I still got terrible emails
from Casper. He was playing the victim, again; his ego had been
bruised, and I was taking the brunt of it. Every day, I made sure
the kids were collected, fed, loved, and had a nice bath and lots of
cuddles. And yes, they could sleep in Mum's bed too. I'd go to
sleep at ten, maybe later. I also needed to talk to Kirsten, Polly,
my parents, my sister, or my auntie Ulla (the provider of bowl
cuts) – anyone who would listen and who could tell me that I
wasn't going mad. Being at the mercy of debt collectors, in my
mind, is mental abuse.

I contacted Casper's family and they simply didn't want to get
involved, offering no help or support for me or the kids. They
abandoned us completely, and we never heard from them again,
apart from Casper's sister, who still imposed distance.

At my lowest ebb, Polly moved in with her kids and her partner, Chey, for the weekend. They looked after the children, while
I worked eighteen-hour days. I was so nervous about an
upcoming wedding that I hardly slept. That morning, I went
down to the kitchen, where Polly was cooking breakfast, and
made a cup of coffee. I farted and shat my pants – it was the most
embarrassing moment. My fragile health meant I could not
control my bowels.

She just said, "Not to worry, darling, at least it can be
washed off."

I suppose her analysis was right – I could wash off my own
shit. It was all the other shit I was having a hard time getting
rid of.

Rubber Face with a Stripper's Name

I kept getting told that I needed to go out, to see grownups, to have sex, to have 'me time'. "You need to have fun!" they said, and, "You need to let your hair down! You deserve it."

I agreed and, before I went to work, I organised a babysitter. Still, I felt guilty. I felt like I was leaving the kids behind.

My first date was at what we called 'The Orange Pub', in Richmond. I remember opening the door and being overwhelmed by the noise of people and the smell of fags (it was, at this time, still legal to smoke inside). The combination scared the shit out of me. I closed the door again and sat on a bench outside. I felt as if I'd never gone out before. I'd been a party girl my whole life, and here I was, sat on a bench outside a pub, my date inside waiting for me.

I went in after twenty minutes of good thoughts and breathing exercises, ordered a large glass of wine, and threw it down in one. That was better. The bartender looked at me as if I was a crazy woman, which really, I couldn't argue with.

My date was, bless him, part of my 'back to dating' process. He tried to be a gentleman, and I told him I found such behaviour boring.

To this, he said, "What, you want me to talk dirty?"

I said, "No, just don't say what you think I want to hear, be yourself."

The conversation was odd, and we got drunk very quickly. Of course, we ended up hammered and having unprotected sex, after lots of what I like to call 'emotional drinking'. All I did was talk about Casper, the affair, my money problems, and my kids. The guy was nodding so much I thought his head would snap off. The next day, I went to Boots and sat in the back of the store, like a school kid, to get the morning after pill. Bravo, Kat! I haven't seen the guy, since – I think he ran away as quickly as he could. Kirsten, who had set it up, never mentioned it again.

Prior to this, I'd already been to the sex clinic, since I'd had no way of knowing how many people Casper had been with in his infidelity. I hadn't felt embarrassed then, but this time, it was agonising. After being called in and peeing in a cup, I walked out with a bag of condoms, feeling like a teenager who didn't know how to handle herself.

The emotional drinking sessions repeated themselves a couple of times. It was quite pathetic, really. The kids would be looked after by a good friend or babysitter and, on some weekends, by their father, who would actually stick to seeing them and have them for a night or two.

I would stand there at a bar, on yet another date that had been set up by a friend, and feel like the sexiest, slimmest woman in the world, but I needed Dutch courage first and, unfortunately, I always got drunk too quickly.

I don't think men really understand how much effort and emotion we single mums put into getting ready for a date. For example: before shaving our legs, armpits, having a Brazilian, and putting sexy underwear on, we prepare ourselves psychologically, thinking positive, calm, cool thoughts. Of course, before we do that, we have to pick up the kids, work on emails, walk the dog, clean the house, and cook dinner. Then, we cuddle the kids (because we already feel super guilty about leaving them). All that, and you want us to wear the suspenders and belts and high heels? I mean, do we ask you to buy a mankini? Washing the dishes is foreplay for many of us women, so men should cut us some slack and focus on what's really important. And that's not just our performance in bed, but also out of bed, and the exhausting tasks we have to finish before we even get to yours.

Finding myself, again, in the new world of being a single parent, was complicated. Being single is hard enough, but with two kids, I found it almost impossible. I was really happy without my ex, but all my trust in men, and in people in general, had left me. As relieved and empowered as I felt to have stood up to Casper and shown my strength, I also felt doubt. I didn't trust anyone – I mean, if I'd chosen the worst person to be my beautiful children's father, how could I be trusted to find someone who was truly good? It was a problem I spent a lot of time talking over with Petra.

Friendships changed drastically and quickly. How I measured up as a mum was, to some, also my identity as a person, but I was still trying to hold on to being the person I was before I'd become a mum, and I found it impossible. I often asked myself, *Who the hell are you?* I'd been failed by the one I'd chosen to have children with, and that had left me battered and bruised. I took the kids through it all, we had survived so far, and now I felt that I couldn't do anything just for myself without being judged. The dating, the friendships: everything had changed. I'd done all the right things, followed my morals and my heart, but I was still questioned by friends: was I a good enough mum? Was I being sensible in my actions? Was I a good friend? Should I be dating in a different way? These were the friends who were all in long-term relationships, and I found we were 'growing apart' as they couldn't comprehend what I was going through. It was a painful process. The truth was, I needed time for myself, and if I spent that time shagging, then so be it. *Why judge me, if I don't mix it with my family life? I'm a good mum and a good friend!*

I milled around on the Ann Summers website, looking at their Rampant Rabbit sex toys, which every one of my girlfriends had told me to get, but I was too scared of the kids finding it, and of the postman judging me, when it came. I was still just 'coming out' as a single mum, and I had to take small steps.

I did start going on more sober dates, and I suppose what you could call 'acceptable' dates. I met a guy through a friend, and we started seeing each other, a little. He came to mine, one night, while the kids were at their father's. We ate dinner, had sex, and had an amazing time.

All night, Rosie sounded really funny, and I wondered if she was protesting at not being able to lie in bed next to me. The next morning, we got up slowly and began tidying up the bed. He told me that he couldn't find the condom, which of course made me run to the toilet, to look for it. I couldn't believe that, finally, I had made a sensible choice, only to have to search around in my tutu, with my leg around my neck, for this bloody condom. No luck. He left, and I had a shower and drove Rosie to Richmond Park.

On my walk, I spoke to Polly on the phone about dating as a single mum and, while telling her how I felt, Rosie started to whine and began almost crawling around. I was freaking out and told Polly that I'd call her back. I ran to Rosie and saw she had a plastic bag hanging out of her bum. I got angry, because she clearly still hadn't learned not to eat everything out of the bin. I stood there, trying to get the bag out of my dog's arse with a stick, thinking I'd hit rock bottom. Suddenly, I saw that the bag was actually a condom – somehow, I'd sunk lower. I was absolutely mortified. I finally got the condom out and stood there with my stick, the condom hanging from the end of it. I looked like I was in a kids' game with a surrender flag. In Denmark, we don't litter, and that principle had stuck with me, so I wandered to the bin, red-faced. Not only did I dump the guy the same day, but I also prayed that Rosie wasn't hurt, and that no vet bills came my way. I didn't want to have to explain what had happened to the vet.

Life went on, and I started to think that I'd rather meet men and have fun than be emotionally available. It was less hassle and, funnily enough, made me very attractive, according to the men I'd met. I wanted nothing from them; no emotional talks, no endless texting, no promises made, just pure and simple fun. I wasn't looking to see if they'd be suitable husbands, boyfriends, providers, or stepfathers. It took all the pressure off.

Some of my friends weren't keen on my new way of dating and thought I needed to grow up. It hit me after meeting up with Sam for a coffee. She'd suggested a blind date with a colleague of hers, and then had turned around, laughed, and said, "Actually, it might not be a good idea. I don't want him to be scared off, or think we're all party animals, like you."

I was deeply hurt. I didn't want to commit because I wasn't ready, and she seemed unable to understand that my decision came from a place of hurt. I'd made a conscious choice and, if that made me seem wild and easy, then I could accept that. She, and others like her, couldn't see what it was like to be a single mother.

I carried on dating and met a semi-professional rugby player, who was also an oil trader. He was tall, broad-shouldered, and very handsome. Rugby players tend to be very posh but mumble and come across as quite butch. We had lots of fun – we always met at his place, so I didn't need to involve him in my life. We went to a pub one night and, smirking, he told me how he'd never been dumped. Now, I liked the guy, but he was no stepfather material. Since I wasn't looking for anything, I dumped him there and then. It felt like a good deed towards the women he'd meet after.

I often looked into the mirror and tried to figure out who I was, which was a tool Petra had given me to get closer to myself. After everything, I suddenly had time to reflect. I had, for a long while, simply forgotten how to do things on my own. Now, after lots of soul searching, sisterhood, family support, talking to friends, and being present with my children, I had woken up and felt the changes. I found that complaining was a waste of time. It's okay to moan and share your problems, but complaining without doing anything is pointless. There's no miracle cure; it takes hard work, and I'm still working on it. I believe I always will be, to some extent.

I shared my dating life with my closest friends. It was fun, and I'd tell them everything. A man I saw for a while (handsome, tall, big muscles, pretty face, and far younger than me) took me out on a date, one night. I was flattered. He had a tattoo sleeve and, as if he was in a Coca Cola advert, was always taking his shirt off to cut the grass on his big lawnmower. After the date, I decided right there and then that he would be my fantasy, but one lived out in reality. We had nothing in common – he had no kids, was seven years younger, and I still wasn't ready, whereas he was looking for a family unit. I made it clear to him that we weren't in the same place, and he accepted it. What was there not to like? We had a laugh and brilliant sex, with no limits. I would tell my friends what he did to me – how he'd swing me up against a wall and take me, and how, in the morning, he'd pop by for a coffee, or book a hotel room with champagne. He would call me and ask me to go and buy the sexiest outfit in Ann Summers, then come around to his place dressed up, so he could take me quickly, during his break. For my friends, my stories were much more fun to listen to than the telly. One day, I spoke to Camilla on the phone, who I hadn't spoken to for ages. I was sitting with a glass of red wine, catching up, laughing, and chatting. She said I was being brave.

I asked her what she meant and she said, "Well, he's younger and built, and you're a mum."

I was stunned that some women saw themselves like this. I wasn't one of them, anymore. I was more confident than ever.

I answered, "I think this young man is lucky. I don't ask anything from him. I give him sex, and I have life experience. I work, and I'm a brilliant mum – where is it exactly that I'm being brave? Is it my hanging tits that measure my bravery? Is it my jelly belly, because I carried twins for nine months? Tell me, where is it that I've been brave?"

She replied, "Oh, you know, it's just that the body changes and, seeing his picture, he looks like a model."

I replied, "You know what? This is what's so wrong with women. Look how shallow we've become. Please, do me a favour: change your attitude, and be strong. I have to go and feed my brave body with some carbohydrates, so we'll speak again soon."

I hung up and was just so disappointed in Camilla. Then again, she was one of those who'd never invited me to events or on family trips, and now, I thought I understood why.

I carried on seeing him, and other men too. Some women saw this as me being slutty. I was on my own path, searching for who I was again, and didn't care too much about any of the people who were judging me. It was all water off a duck's back. I had no time for people who judged others because of their gender.

On a personal level, I did sometimes struggle with feelings of wanting to take a relationship further because of the loneliness and false hope. Of course, I knew it wasn't possible, and I pushed the feelings away. I needed more time and, if I wasn't ready, there was no point in introducing anyone to my kids which I had not done.

School Runs, Trainers, and Pink
Legwarmers

❧❧❧

S lowly, I established a routine and started breathing normally. I was always under pressure, but I understood that this wouldn't go away for at least a few years, and I would simply have to accept it.

The kids were now starting school, and it meant I had emails from the school every freaking day. In Denmark, you don't start until you're six, so it took me a while to adjust to my babies being in school at less than five years old. The school was just around the corner from my house, at least, so I could walk them there in just five minutes. Now and again, I got pulled back up a stress level when the car wouldn't start, or a tax bill arrived, or someone I owed money to became impatient, but I dealt with it. After much research and effort, I knew I would be okay.

I started saving some money and so, one afternoon, I had lunch with Polly at a small, cheap pub in Richmond. The wine hit me so quickly that I decided to take a cab home. It stopped in front of my house. The sun was out, summer was here, and I felt tipsy, but great. I was smiling again; it felt good to just be allowed to have a drink on a Friday afternoon with a friend. I walked over the grass and my heel got stuck. I fell over, nearly knocked myself out feeling dizzy, and I remember opening my eyes and the grass being so soft, and my body being so heavy, that I thought, *I'll just lay here for a minute, resting.* My neighbour was looking at me through her window, and I felt the judgement creeping up again. I got up with a sore head and walked into the house, making a cup of tea and then getting changed to pick up the kids. There was always a challenge around the corner, so I decided not to care about the neighbour and what she might say. I just carried on with my day.

I sometimes felt like a PA or a chauffeur to my kids. I ran a hundred miles in order for them to fit in and have friends, and it meant that I worked just as hard, if not harder, as a mum than at my actual job. It was so draining that I often wanted to go back to my red wine period; no pressure, no judgement, just kids being kids while I drank my glasses of wine, free to fall asleep not worrying about tomorrow. I felt slightly heartbroken about not being able to afford all the school clubs, as these amounted to hundreds of pounds, with all the various forms of gear and instruments. What happened to just playing sticks and stones in the back yard, or roller skating and creating dens out of branches?

It was hard, and I had no support from Casper. He told me he was rebuilding his life in Holland, now. Carolina had been left with his £3000 debt, but she was sure he'd pay it back and still loved him, so they were still in contact, and she visited him often. I spent no more time trying to figure him out. I just said small prayers to myself that he would keep his promises and visit the kids often. It was out of my hands.

One of the things that helped me survive was the morning school runs. Mothers have so much going on, behind closed doors. Talking to other mums in the morning gave me some relief – I wasn't the only one shouting at my kids about tidying up, or being too noisy, for example. It gave me a fresh perspective on myself too. None of us are perfect, even the mums or women who judge you. I came to meet two mums, Iris and Robyn. They were to become close friends, later in life. We had kids in the same class, and our friendships blossomed over the school years.

When I walked the kids to school, I had a huge need to listen in on other people, purely to distract myself from my own problems. There were mornings where I would listen to the mums moaning about not having time to wash, or clean the house, because of all the cakes they had to bake for charity. They were tired of their husbands working so many hours and never seeing them – apparently, they just bought their kids lots of stuff: iPads, iPods, new trainers, trips to Legoland, you name it. Okay, I understood; it can be hard, but pick your battles – that's all I'm saying. Surrender to the fact that maybe things aren't that bad, and that perhaps it's the focus that needs changing. You have an income, another set of hands on the weekends, three holidays a year, and you don't have to be the only one worrying about bills, keeping the kids fed, etc. So yes, these were the mums I stayed away from. Not as an insult, but because their ego couldn't recognise the abundance they already had. Unreasonable, maybe, but that was my world. I wasn't a victim, but going through what I had, I couldn't understand their choices of life's battles.

We often just stood outside the school gates talking, as everyone always had somewhere to be. Some of the stories that got told were so funny and reminded me of the humour of motherhood, which was lovely when we were all drained and just wanted to go on that one-month holiday to a desert island.

One such story was told by Robyn, who had five boys and a husband. They both worked full-time and juggled their working lives with parenting. One day, she told me, she got up even earlier than normal, baked some beautiful fresh bread, put the jam, butter, and cheese on the table, told the boys that breakfast was ready, and went up to the bathroom to treat herself with a nice, long shower. When she came back, she found the bread untouched and all the kids sitting around the table with gadgets. The youngest was pretending that his willy was a massive dinosaur attacking him. She was stunned and asked why on Earth they hadn't eaten the bread.

One of her older sons looked at her like she was from Mars and replied, "There are no knives on the table, Mum."

I hated being alone with my thoughts, and so I started talking to anyone and anything. This was how my school morning runs started. I was surprised by how many people I connected with on those runs to and from school.

Iris told me that she came home one Saturday to find her husband and kids waiting to welcome her in the hallway. They announced that they had cleaned the whole house for her. Truly, she was not amazed. She told them that she wasn't aware that she was the cleaner, and that she was happy that they could, from now on, take over, as she was now certain they could all clean. Then she had turned around and gotten back into the car, switched her phone off, and driven herself to a restaurant, where she'd ordered a massive steak and a glass of red wine. When she later came home, the kids and husband were slightly embarrassed and had gotten the message.

Another mum, who had two boys and a kid in the same class as my twins, said that her oldest son had told her how much he hated her for not being allowed to stay home from school and play video games. It was, apparently, a constant battle. One day, she lost it and placed him in front of the computer to watch a documentary about starving children in Africa.

After twenty minutes, she looked at him and said, "You want to compare?"

Not pedagogically correct, but hey, he got the message.

Even Polly told me a story about her and Chey going to a festival with their family. Chey had gotten tired and felt unwell, and Polly had suggested he take some painkillers and go back to the tent for some sleep. She'd stayed out for a few more hours with other friends and kids. When she and the kids came back, they had found him with two paracetamol in his ears and no earplugs in sight. It turned out that he'd swallowed them. It had been a difficult task to explain to the kids what had really happened, and that their dad hadn't been that drunk.

It was good to hear these stories, as it made me feel that the world around me was more human, and not as judgmental as some people made me believe it was.

My own mum had a story to share too. Once, she'd gone to stay at a hotel somewhere in Europe with my dad. They got tipsy at dinner, so they came back to the hotel and went to bed. My mum woke up needing the toilet and walked into what she thought were the toilets, realising only when she looked up that she had ended up in the hotel hallway, completely naked. She dragged a nearby pot plant in front of her and frantically knocked until my dad opened the door. Even better, Dad was just annoyed about being woken up and asked her what the hell she was doing naked in the hallway. It took her years to tell me that story.

Saying you're lonely out loud has almost become taboo, today – people will run away from you because, god forbid, they have to entertain you out of guilt or pity. Loneliness is meant to be an emotion, like sadness, but it has unfortunately become something we suffer from, instead of a feeling we deal with. I would rather deal with it, learn how to live with it, and make the choice to not feel lonely as much as possible. I also make the choice to be there for other people when they feel like this. I know that many people are lonely in their relationships – this, to me, seems like a much worse place to be, but it's not a competition! My measure for my personal success grew from believing I was a good parent, friend, daughter, and sister.

The more my mental health and spirit improved, the more my life did the same. The things that have happened in my life so far have made a huge mark on me. I know now that whatever is thrown at me, I will survive it. I'm not afraid to feel sad. Don't get me wrong, it's a fucker, particularly when it's heartbreak, but I also know I'll get over it, if I allow myself to process it.

Kirsten said this to me when I felt very down one day: "I have learned to find beauty in very small places but, most of all, learned to surrender battles I am not capable of winning. It can make one feel very old and tremendously boring, but so calm and grateful, as well. Don't think I got there without a huge amount of screaaaaaaaaammiiiiing."

I carried on screaming in the bushes regularly, and I knew that my friend understood me, even if no one else did. I also started making changes, getting some freelance staff to help me at work. It meant less money for me and the kids, but more time together. We'd walk Rosie, cook, or do something creative. I stopped arguing with Casper about visiting the kids or paying support, because he clearly didn't want to help, and there was no reason to get myself frustrated. Trying to fight with Casper was like holding hot stones in my hand – I was the only one getting burned.

I started slowly getting ready for a new relationship. I started believing that I could be happy and that someone would love me, with kids and all. I realised that, while being a single mum was an important part of my life, it didn't define me. The future was ahead.

Love Is

I was finally in a good place. I'd slowly gotten back on my feet, and I was actually earning good money. I was still paying Casper's debts off, and would be until the end, but I had accepted this, as I had no alternatives. The kids were thriving in school and, though Casper was sinking further and further into the background, I was happy at how peaceful our unit had become.

I started going out more with my girlfriends, including Polly, Kirsten, and the mums at the kids' school, Iris and Robyn, who were trying to persuade me to meet someone for a serious relationship. I had accidently told them I was "ready for a relationship, I think" one night, and they took it upon themselves to find me a man.

We were in a bar in Richmond, all dressed up. We always had a good time; most of my girlfriends had husbands so, for them, it was just about the night out, not pulling men. This guy came up to me, and all he did was smirk and talk to me in a really weird accent.

"You alright?" he slurred. I wasn't really interested.

"Where's your accent from?" I asked.

"I'm Welsh, and you?"

"I'm Danish, but I live here in Richmond."

I tried to casually walk away, but my new mum friend, Iris, stopped me and asked the guy for his number. Iris put his number into my phone and told me that I needed a decent man. He smiled, and I could tell that he was drunk. He said he was celebrating his birthday. I congratulated him, and we went on to a club. I left him there, and our group went to a bar and danced all night. On my way home, I got a text from this guy, who said his name was 'Robert'. 'Hey,' the text read, 'was nice to meet you. Would love to have a drink with you one day.'

I didn't reply, as I was tired and on my way to meet the babysitter.

He texted me over the next couple of days, and I decided to go out with him. We met at the pub and, when I saw him, I realised he was actually quite good-looking. He had black, swirly hair and was tall and quite broad-shouldered. He had piercing blue eyes, heart-shaped lips, and looked slightly like a dark-haired James Dean. His dress sense was smart, but casual. Unfortunately, I didn't feel any attraction to him – not because of him, but because I was still numb. Frustratingly, we actually hit it off straightaway. He told me he couldn't remember how I'd looked, but his mates had said I was a looker, so they'd told him to pursue a date. I wasn't impressed, but it was just how these things went at bars, so I didn't take it personally. He'd bought me a glass of wine and, when I finished that, he bought a bottle, which is always a good sign. We got drunk and had so much fun. I think we both felt like we'd known each other for much longer than just a few hours. He was funny and interesting, and I started to love his accent.

We slept together on that first night. I felt I had nothing to lose, as I didn't see us being together. He was six years younger than me, and I was in no hurry to meet someone. The numbness was a defence mechanism I still hadn't conquered. As I was in contact with two other men, at this point, I didn't even feel the need to question what this could become. As one of the girls had said, it was important that I didn't seem desperate and made sure I had "a few different candles lit." It would make me feel in control and, as long as I didn't promise anything, my integrity would remain intact.

Robert was born in Wales, had a big sister, and had lived in Richmond for a year. He was planning to be an architect, and was working on building sites as a surveyor while he studied. He lived with two other professionals, and he was actually quite shy. He was a typical man in terms of his interests and sense of humour; he watched football and rugby nonstop and made comments such as, "Going to a pub, watching a game, and picking up a curry on your way home is really all a man needs." He was falling for me, just as I was for him. I think it was a massive surprise for us both. The numbness was fading, and I realised it had happened naturally.

I called things off with the other men. The model got really upset. I'm not sure why, as we were never serious, and he'd told me that he wasn't emotionally available. I started to understand that, as soon as I wasn't asking men for anything, they'd give me the world; it was only when I wanted some commitment that they'd stammer, "It's a lot of responsibility" or, "I'm not sure if I'm ready." Anyway, I told him I was sorry, but he sent several angry messages, and we ended on bad terms.

Robert and I had started dating seriously, and I was giving into him completely. We became one of those annoying couples you see who can't take their eyes off each other. Everything the other one said was just "so true and so funny."

One day, he decided to cook me dinner. We were at the stage where I just couldn't wait to see him, and I had butterflies in my stomach. It was crazy how fast things were moving. I arrived at his flat and he opened the door.

"Hey, babe, so good to see you."

He looked good, he smelled good, and he ran out to hug and

kiss me on the staircase. The front door slammed behind him, and his face just froze. He tried to open it, but it was locked. We tried to open the door in different ways, but without any success. He left me on the staircase and went around the building. I could hear him crawling through his kitchen window and smashing things that must have been on the window ledge, and he finally came to the door and opened it from the inside. We couldn't stop laughing, and I tried to convince him to just go to a pub and get some grub, but he was adamant that we had to get back into the flat. When I walked into his living room, I understood why. He'd lit about fifty candles and placed them all over the room. He'd set a table, sorted flowers, and cooked all day. The evening was our first step into what would become a deep and beautiful relationship. It was truly romantic.

Everything was spoken about. All our inner demons, all our fears, all our dreams. I think he thought I was crazy in many ways, but he admired the fact that I was a girl from Denmark who had created something for herself. He would tell me often how he absolutely worshipped the ground I walked on, just for being such a survivor. I was the perfect woman for him, and he loved the fact that I wouldn't shy away from banter. I wasn't sensitive to much, and often felt like saying to many girls, "Lighten the fuck up." Many men, I suppose, wouldn't like this, and would prefer someone more ladylike who was still a whore in bed. Still, we decided that he shouldn't meet the kids until he and I were as prepared as we could be.

A few more months went by, and I met his friends, who were all great. Most of them were in serious relationships, and were at roughly the same place as I was in life. Robert turned out to be quite a jealous partner. He didn't like my Facebook profile picture, which showed me in a bikini. He called it 'promiscuous'. I was just proud that, after having twins, my body was still looking sort of decent, and I wanted to celebrate rather than hide it away.

One night, I had to go to the Groucho Club in Soho to meet with Emma, a new friend I'd made through work. She was a PA to one of my famous clients, Vivienne Westwood. I arranged to meet Robert afterwards in Richmond. The kids were with their grandparents, who were visiting.

All the PA's got really drunk, that night, and I had to help one of them home in a cab so that she wouldn't lose her job. It was a messy but fun night. Famous actors were there, and I chatted with several of them. It was fun looking at their faces in the flesh, instead of on the screen – it was like a museum experience. After what I'd been through, I had put my life into perspective – and besides, it'd never been in my personality to be in awe of famous people. They were all made the same way, and all came from the same part of their mothers as the rest of us.

By the time I was on my way back to Richmond to meet Robert, I was running late. I was sitting in a cab with Emma (who was really drunk) and a famous actor. They were headed to Emma's house for a party and, as she lived close to Richmond, it made sense to share a cab. I was trying to text Robert that I was running late, but wasn't too worried, as he was with his football mates and had wanted to meet up late anyway. I was planning to stay at Robert's and go home early in the morning, as I had a meeting the next day. The taxi stopped, and Emma and the actor got out, trying vigorously, but in vain, to get me to join them for the party.

I looked at Emma and said, "Jesus, Em', pull yourself together, woman!"

I rushed to the bar Robert was in. He was quite drunk and stood near the bar with all his mates. He could hardly say 'hello' and was cold to me, and I felt instantly repulsed. All the other guys were just as drunk, but they all gave me a hug, which was nice, considering Robert and I had only been seeing each other for a few months. We got a few drinks and I tried to speak to Robert.

"I'm really sorry I was late, but I had to get this PA home safe, and then I waited for Emma to get into a cab with her date."

He responded with, "I thought you were standing me up."

I said I would never do that and gave him a hug. I smiled and went to talk to his mates, in an effort to get to know them. An hour or so later, I couldn't find Robert, and we all got a bit concerned. His flatmate, Benny, found his jacket and wallet, so we thought he must have gone outside for a smoke. I went outside, but Robert was nowhere to be seen. Benny asked me to go with him to see whether Robert was at the flat. All the other boys joined us, and we walked across the bridge, tipsy and happily singing songs.

We found Robert lying on his bed, and I asked him if he wanted me to stay. He was so drunk that he just mumbled something, so I lay down and fell asleep next to him. Later on in the night, I woke up suddenly. Robert was standing by the bed, pissing on my legs. Well, he'd now joined the drunk men's pissing club. My father once did this, in a drunken state, but instead chose to piss in my mum's antique piano. He had to clean the keys the next day, and I don't think I'll ever forget the sound of the piano as he did. Robert even farted and scratched his arse, as if he was in the toilet. I was mortified, and yet I wasn't sure if I should wake him up, as I wasn't ready for this kind of embarrassment. Not to mention, he had made it clear that he preferred women who farted in silence. I moved my legs and he lay back down, as if nothing had happened. I carefully got up, got a blanket, and curled up against the wall, seriously considering going home, but I knew my parents would have heart attacks if I arrived back at one in the morning. I fell back to sleep and woke up at six. I tried to wake up Robert and started giggling.

"How's the pisshead?"

I thought it was a really funny joke, but he just looked at me, visibly confused.

"Why is the bed wet?" were his first words.

"Maybe because you pissed in the bed, last night?"

He looked at me as if I was from Mars and then got angry with me. I felt rage rising up inside. Not only had this man left me in a bar, but he'd given my calves a good warm soak, and now *he* was angry with *me?*

I took my stuff and walked out, saying, "Go fuck yourself, Mr. Connor."

I walked home (we only lived a mile apart) and, on the way, realised that I'd really fallen for the man. My heart was aching, and I could tell I was trying to run as fast as I could from this feeling. Getting hurt just wasn't something I was sure I could cope with. I knew relationships were one long negotiation, but I didn't know if I was ready to negotiate about anything.

I walked into my house, having failed to make any final decision beyond never speaking to the wanker again. I cuddled my kids, played the 'I'm fine' card to my parents, had a shower, and went to the meeting I had scheduled with wedding clients.

He texted me a few hours later, saying he felt really stupid. He asked me if we could meet and said that he understood if I wanted him to piss off. Of course, I melted at the first text, and as the kids were home safe, I swung by his flat on my way home. He was on his way to Wales and spent a good five minutes apologising profusely. It was all good – we had survived our first fight. I went back to spend the weekend with the kids and my parents, and he went off to Wales (after, of course, some make-up sex). I was already excited about seeing him when he returned.

It got more serious, and we had a hard time not seeing each other every day. He could work from home, so I would go over when the kids were in school, and we had a lot of river picnics. Slowly, I began to leave my identity as a single mum behind me. One day, I was just watching Robert, and I realised that I wanted to spend the rest of my life with him. I wanted to love him when he was a prick, love him when he loved me back, and grow old with him. I trusted him completely.

Before we'd met, he'd committed to a wedding holiday in Turkey with his best mate, who still lived in Wales and who I hadn't yet met. He would be away for nearly three weeks. We both suffered, and the ache I felt was all-consuming. He phoned twice, sometimes three times a day from Turkey, to say that he was thinking of coming home early. Of course, he wouldn't – he was the best man, but it was clear to us both that we were completely in love.

When he came home, I went to his place and he opened the door, pulled me in, and kissed me. He told me how much he loved me. He was ready to meet the kids, and he couldn't imagine a life without me. I was so happy, I could have exploded. It was better than a proposal. He had said out loud exactly what he wanted.

We started planning to meet each other's families. Sometimes, I couldn't breathe because I felt claustrophobic. Things were going well, but I still had fears, though I dealt with them. We women are much better at processing all this with the help of our girlfriends, while men go through it alone, thinking that only they feel suffocated and scared.

Pepper and Magnus were so excited to meet Robert. It was a warm summer's day, and we decided to have dinner in our small garden. The kids and I were cooking when he rang the doorbell. Rosie went nuts, and he must have felt as if he was arriving at a circus. He was visibly nervous, and I hugged him and sat him down with us at the garden table. After we had chatted for a bit, and the dog had calmed down, I went into the kitchen to finish the food, and he sat with the kids in the garden. I opened the window above the sink so I could speak to them while preparing the food. Pepper was testing Robert by seeing if he could spell 'Rottweiler', and Magnus was trying to show Robert his Lego figures, while explaining how to put them together. Magnus loved having a male in the house, and Pepper loved the fact that she could play teacher with someone else, as this was her favourite role. Even Rosie was happy to be scratched behind her ear by another person.

Things went well that evening, and he started coming over more often. On Mother's Day, he bought gifts for the kids to give to me, and the kids were completely confused, as they had never seen that type of kindness or thoughtfulness from their own dad. It was such a beautiful transition, from there being just the three of us to the four of us.

Then it was my turn to meet his family, in Wales. His big sister, Joanie, her husband, David, and their two kids. She was a teacher, but was out of work and currently focused on looking after their young daughters. Joanie was thirty-eight, the same age as me. I was also going to meet his parents, Maria and Michael. Michael was a builder who had worked really hard, since they'd had Joanie at the young age of only sixteen. He was from a tight family unit and was apparently very morally correct. They stood by each other, when things got tough. All in all, his family sounded amazing, and I loved the fact that they were from Wales – partly because my favourite series at that time was *Gavin & Stacey*, but also because I loved the idea of us visiting Wales and showing the kids a different culture.

Polly and Chey came for the weekend with their son, Daryl, and their new baby daughter, Daisy, to look after Magnus, Pepper, and Rosie. She arrived on Friday, after school had ended.

"How are you, love?" she asked. She was my closest friend, and I knew she loved me. We would go to the world's end for each other, and she could read me like a book.

"I'm so nervous, Polly, I might shit my pants again." We looked at each other and laughed out loud. "Truly, Polly," I continued, "I know this is it – I'm meeting my future parents-in-law, and I can't wait. I just hope they like me."

"Of course they will," said Polly. "You're kind, you're a great mum, you're hardworking, and you've done it all by yourself." I hugged her and then cuddled the kids' goodbye – I'd said I had some business in Wales to attend to, and mentioned that we would meet Robert's parents only briefly, because if they'd known we were going for a whole weekend, they'd have wanted to come. It was important that Robert and I did this on our own, first. It could be that they hated me and ended our relationship. The guilt was inevitable; something I'd learned, by now.

The drive took about three hours. I was so nervous that I had to have cigarettes, even though I'd stopped smoking years ago. I knew it was a big deal, as Robert told me that he'd never introduced a girlfriend to his parents, before. I sat in the car, watching him drive. I touched his cheek and felt this beautiful feeling gush through my body – this was it. I had found my soulmate.

We were driving over the Severn Bridge, towards Joanie and David's place, looking out at the beautiful views. Robert's dad, brother-in-law, sister, and two nieces would be waiting for us. When we pulled into the drive, his mum opened the front door and ran out. Robert got out of the car and hugged her.

She then came over to my side of the car, opened the door, and said in her beautiful Welsh accent, "Come out, Kat, I've been dying to meet you!" She smiled. "I've been so nervous. It's a big thing to finally meet you." She was tiny and pretty, with a flair of '70s style about her. I instantly liked her.

I smiled, but my mouth was so dry that I couldn't speak. I just hugged her and stumbled out, murmuring how it was great to be here.

We went inside, and Robert knelt down to greet his nieces. They were happy to see him and clambered all over him. I got pulled out to the garden, and Joanie and Maria sat me down straightaway and poured me a large glass of red wine. It was nearly filled to the rim, and I was worried that my hands might shake so much that I'd spill it on the table cloth. Nevertheless, I needed the courage, so I took a really big gulp. Joanie was just as tiny as her mum, with a '60s bob and a similar style. I loved it, and we clicked straightaway.

It turned out I needn't have worried; Joanie and Maria were so nice. Joanie spoke with a soft voice and a heavy Welsh accent. It was a blissful afternoon, and we had a barbecue and drank wine as we spoke about our children. Michael came out and made me feel totally at ease by speaking to me about running one's own business, and he also told me many funny stories about Robert, much to Robert's embarrassment. I'd totally clicked with his family, and Robert told me afterwards that they loved me.

We woke up early and had morning sex on the noisiest fold-out couch I'd ever laid in. I kept hushing Robert, as the last thing I wanted to be remembered for was having rabbit sex in his sister's house. I got up and went for a shower, and we all had breakfast. Later that day, Robert and I drove down to the Gower Peninsula. We had lunch in a restaurant with a beautiful view and, in the evening, we'd arranged to meet his friends.

I was frantic about what to wear. I was insecure, remembering that I was six years older than Robert, and it didn't help that he tried to reassure me by saying he'd always dated older girls; he'd just never introduced anyone to his friends, before.

His parents drove us to a pub in the middle of nowhere. I was wearing a black top and jeans – I looked good, felt good, and was nervous in a good way. Robert held my hand in front of the pub and turned to look at me.

He looked so proud as he said, "I love you, and I can't wait for you to meet my friends."

He kissed me, and we went in. The pub was really old and scabby, and there were flies hovering over my head. The bartender had the biggest fake eyelashes on and massive boobs. She wore bright pink lipstick and blue eyeshadow, and her cleavage was so prominent that I wondered why she even bothered to wear the top. She was awesome. I called it 'personality'! The men all turned to look at us, as we walked in, and I saw that no one was dressed up – it was all jeans, builders' clothes, t-shirts, and bellies spilling out over waistbands. All in all, it was a *Gavin &*

Stacey moment. I went to sit, and Robert went to the bar. While I was waiting for him, this tall, skinny girl walked in with heavily highlighted, helmet-shaped hair and loads of jewellery dangling from her arms and neck.

"Where is she?" she shouted at Robert, as she frantically looked around the room. Her eyes caught mine, and she said, "Bloody hell, Robert, she's way too pretty for you."

She smiled. Behind her was a shy, red-faced man. He just waved at me and joined Robert at the bar.

The girl, Zoe, sat next to me and said, "Kat, you're gorgeous, are those tits of yours real?"

The atmosphere was set for the evening, as more of Robert's friends began arriving.

Later that night, when the pubs were closed, we were invited to Zoe and her husband Dave's house. Having more drinks and getting to know each other better, Robert confessed to his best mate, Dave, that he wanted us to get married. It wasn't a proposal, but we had spoken about it before – we'd have the reception in a small pub, serve fish and chips, and I'd have a stunning dress and lots of flowers. Dave's jaw was on the floor. He'd never heard Robert even say he was committed, let alone that he was in love. It was so intense. I had sat with Zoe, who was now quite blurry and, for three hours, listened to a story about the same bridesmaid, who hadn't wanted to wear a dress she'd bought for her and Dave's wedding, which had been the wedding in Turkey that had taken Robert away for nearly three weeks. The news coming out of Robert rendered her silent for the first time. They cheered by opening up champagne, and Zoe immediately started talking about what kind of wedding dress I wanted. I nudged Robert and told him that we needed to get home.

The next day, we woke up and had breakfast with his parents. We were all still laughing and his mum, in particular, was someone I really got on with.

Finally, the weekend was over. On our return journey, we bought souvenirs for the kids, such as Welsh flags and chocolates.

We came back on the same day Andy Murray won the Wimbledon final, and when we entered the house, Polly and Chey had champagne waiting for us, to celebrate Murray's win. We all got a bit tipsy, and the kids were having a blast. Rosie was barking with delight, and after Polly and Chey had left, I cuddled the kids to bed, telling them how excited everyone in Wales was to meet them. We rolled into bed exhausted and happy. We'd planned for Robert to move in on his next lease renewal, which was months away, and agreed that there was no point in rushing anything. We knew we wanted to be together.

Weeks went on, then months. We had our fights, but they were never scary – we knew we were staying together, and so we worked through them.

My parents came over for Christmas and New Year's Eve. We'd planned for Robert's family to stay at the house, with the twins and my parents at a house they'd borrowed from some of my neighbours, who were away on holiday. I stayed with Robert in his flat-share – 'The Den', we called it. I didn't really know how to introduce our two families, but it all felt so normal, so right. Robert and I had done our shopping together, cooking together, and organising together, and we both knew it was a practice period for when we finally moved in together.

We had a great time, and I introduced herring and snaps to Christmas dinner, Danish style. I warned Robert and his parents that we have a thing called being 'snapsed' – it's our word for when the Danish drinks we serve with the herring ('snaps') suddenly get to you. They shrugged and said they could handle it – after all, they were Welsh.

My father added, "We sophisticated parents are capable of handling a bit of snaps, don't you think, my darling daughter?"

I shrugged, as he was always a joker in company, and I blamed him for my own sense of humour. I invited everyone to the table.

The snaps got to everyone. My father, on his way across the road, ended up hanging from a ladder, on the roof of a van, and Robert had to get him down and put him to bed. Maria and Michael were already in bed, but Maria fell out, slipped on a plate she'd brought up, and created an egg-shaped bump on her forehead. Worse, Michael was sick. I found him running into the toilet in his pants, trying to stop himself from throwing up. My mum was already asleep in her house, and I was the only one who had held back. Robert was so drunk that he collapsed on the couch; I had to take his shoes off and put a blanket over him. It was, all in all, exactly how we Danes celebrate a Danish Christmas lunch, or 'julefrokost'. The kids and I cleaned up and watched some telly with Robert, who was snoring next to us. I felt a breeze of happiness just from us all being together.

For New Year's, David, Joanie, Chloe, and Amy joined us, and we went for some Indian food at a local restaurant. My father was showing off by eating a vindaloo, and David and Michael, of course, followed in his footsteps. We finished the celebrations in the house and let off fireworks for the kids. Joanie and Maria pulled me aside to tell me that they had never seen Robert so in love. We had a few secret cigarettes in the shed and went back into the house, where we danced and drank past midnight, cheering the New Year in, singing *Auld Lang Syne*, and all holding hands in a chain.

The Welsh and the Danes had bonded, and we started organising for my parents to visit Wales, and for Robert's family to visit my parents' French house. Maria was afraid of flying, so we convinced her to either take some Valium, with a Bloody Mary, or start hypnotherapy.

Spring was on its way and, unfortunately, it was a tough year for me, wedding-wise. The bookings weren't coming in as regularly, and I started to struggle financially, again. My mood changed as I was under so much pressure. One night, I was really tired, and Robert wanted sex.

I just said, "Make it quick, I've got to get up early," and he got really offended.

I understood and apologised the next day, but I'd been absolutely knackered. He knew I was having a hard time, and we started to hit some rough ground. He couldn't cope with me not always being on top form, and I didn't have a magic wand to make things better. I couldn't give him the attention I'd been able to, before, and I tried to explain that I needed him to put me under a little less pressure, in terms of what he wanted, or expected, from me. We kind of managed, but I still felt a great pressure to be better than I was and, for the first time, I saw a weakness in Robert. I needed him to be strong and not to take my exhausted detachment personally. I spoke to Polly about our few weeks of not being great.

"You just need to be patient with him," she said. "After all, he's a man, and lots of them aren't as strong as women; they need much more attention."

I agreed with her and stayed strong, because I knew he was struggling with me being under pressure and back to a place where I was struggling, every month, to pay the bills.

A few months later, another of Robert's friends was getting married, and we went to Wales. I had a Vivienne Westwood dress, which I'd borrowed from Emma, and I couldn't wait to just get away, breathe, and put things behind me a little. Polly and Chey were helping with the kids, and Rosie, again. Neither Sam nor Camilla had the capacity to do these things, as it was too much to ask from them, so I counted my blessings for having a friend like Polly, who allowed me these breaks. I brought some sexy underwear and planned not to talk about my struggling business. I wanted Robert and I to have a break.

At the wedding, Robert was the best man, and he was so nervous about his speech that he became irritable. I knew he wasn't in a great place either, professionally speaking, as his responsibilities at work were changing. We were staying at his parent's house, and they were coming too, as they had known the groom, Mike, since he was a kid. As soon as I walked in, I was greeted with a hug and a glass of wine. We all seemed to relax straightaway. We had great food and great company, and we decided to go to bed early. Robert and I had the best lovemaking session we'd had for ages, that night.

In the morning, we got ready for the wedding. Robert wasn't as nervous, now, and I'd had a call from Polly letting me know that the kids were fine.

We arrived at the wedding, which was at the Hilton hotel in Llanelli's town centre, with Robert's parents. All of Robert's London friends had driven over for the wedding, and we had a great start to the day. The ceremony was a typical Welsh affair – purple ties and waistcoats, fake eyelashes hailing the sun, enough hairspray to start a bonfire – I loved every minute of it. Nobody gave a monkey about what anyone else thought; they were who they were. I loved the honesty of these people, the genuine culture – what you saw was what you got.

The ceremony was very emotional. Mike had recently lost his father, and the bride, Susie, had been ill with serious stomach problems. Both had now come out the other side, and so there was even more to celebrate. Zoe had spotted me and threw herself into the chair next to mine.

"So, Kat, you the next one?"

I looked at her but didn't answer. I think Robert's earlier stress had made me tense, and I had my own shit going on with work. Marrying him was the last thing I wanted to think about, right now. That said, he looked stunning in his suit, and when I watched him give Mike the ring at the altar, I fell even more deeply in love with him and couldn't wait to kiss him after the ceremony.

At the reception, we had loads to drink. The wedding photographer was all sweaty and red-faced and had a big belly. He kept taking his handkerchief out to wipe the sweat from his forehead.

There was still some time until the ceremony room turned into the wedding breakfast room, so people got drunk instead.

I was standing with Robert's parents, when his mum asked, "You alright, Kat? You seem quiet."

I answered, "I'm okay, Maria, just quite tough at home, with work. We just had a stressful start to the week, as Robert hasn't been able to sleep, because of the speech and work. We've just been a bit tense."

"You know, my Robert can be a bit of a prick, Kat – it's my fault for spoiling him, but I'm sure you can handle him."

I smiled and hugged her. I truly loved this woman.

"Well said, Maria. I just hope we'll have a great evening."

At that moment, someone shouted and pointed out the window. We saw, through the glass, a huge bus arriving outside. One by one, the Liverpool team came out. Robert was so excited, and I asked him if he wanted Daniel Agger's autograph, as he played on the team. He nodded eagerly. I ran out in my Vivienne Westwood dress, quite tipsy by now, and asked Agger, in Danish, for his autograph. We ended up chatting quite a bit, once he told me he was from Frederiksberg, the same place as me. Robert was stunned and, finally, he smiled. We walked back, and he proudly showed the boys the autograph and told everyone how I'd spoken in Danish to Agger.

"Well," I said, "you just have to tell a man what you want, and he'll give it to you."

Robert's face completely changed – he looked more embarrassed than happy. I wasn't fazed, as I'd had a few glasses of wine. He hadn't lit the fuse on my tampon yet, but he was getting close.

Finally, the wedding dinner was served, and I ended up sitting with Robert's parents and many of his friends. Robert sat with the bride and groom, at the top table. I was still playing the supportive girlfriend and kept sending him thumbs-ups, air kisses, and smiles. I mouthed, 'You'll be okay.'

His mates were fantastic during dinner. They told funny

stories about being wrapped naked in cling film on holidays, and who did what to who. His parents had heard it all before, but nonetheless, it was all quite amusing.

Robert's speech rolled around, and he stood up to talk. Everyone laughed in the right places, and he seemed confident, funny, and serious too. I softened up, listening to him, and felt proud when everyone clapped afterwards. After dinner, I went out with Robert and his two best mates, Mike and Dave. We were quite drunk, and they asked me to tell them the story of Robert weeing in bed. I told the story, complete with a bad, "He really pissed me off," joke, and both Mike and Dave laughed.

"Oh, I've pissed in so many cupboards I've lost count, mate, join the club," Dave said.

We went back inside, and I noticed that Robert was tense again. He kind of ignored me when I went to give him a kiss. I couldn't figure out why he was being so moody.

Later, we went out for a cigarette, and he suddenly told me he thought I was making him look like a fool.

"I mean, if you want to put me down, that's the way to do it. I'm not interested in being with someone who wants to make me feel like shit."

I was astounded – I had no idea where it was coming from.

"I just went along with your friends' questions!" I said. "I'm at your friend's wedding, and I don't need this shit, right now."

I could feel the anger boiling in me. I had never in my life put this man down, but he sure as hell was doing his best to get me down, and it was working. I was standing in Wales at a stranger's wedding, with one of his mate's wives gabbing in my ear about hot footballers and telling me how she was open to the idea of an open relationship, but *I* was the one putting *him* down.

"I tell you, Mr. Robert Connor: first, swallow your pride, and then listen very carefully. You must be the dumbest, most self-centred dick walking the planet, right now, and I will save you from any more distress by booking a room at this hotel. Perhaps then you can go home and sleep in your mum's bed, and she can stroke your head while you suck your thumb and just be really happy that you didn't shit the bed, because I tell you, that story would have some meat on it..."

I turned and headed back to the hotel, leaving Robert alone on the pavement outside. All the little annoying things had come up to the surface, and I'd vented all my anger at him. I was here, without my kids and on his terms, and it infuriated me that he hadn't looked after me. We were both under a lot of pressure, and we must have looked like the typical arguing wedding couple.

I stomped into the hotel's reception and tried to book a room to make sure that Robert knew I was serious about my intentions, but while I was waiting for service, Robert stopped me. I think he was actually surprised by my reaction and my anger. I was slowly showing on the outside that I was drained, and that it was hard being a perfect girlfriend, with perfect kids and a perfect house. I just wanted him to carry me, for a while, and he was unable to. Perhaps I had also made it impossible for him to carry me, or to even understand that I was feeling as thin-skinned as I was. It was as if I had to roleplay as Superwoman. I started sobbing in Robert's arms. The thought went through my mind that maybe I wanted the peace of my own room, after all.

The next morning, we made up. He rolled over in our bed and stroked my face. I was sad and didn't understand his behaviour. Where had his sense of humour gone?

I asked him, "Why did you flip out on me?"

He answered, "I'm vulnerable, with you. I always feel that you could do better than me."

It wasn't the first time we'd had this conversation.

"Robert, I love you, I want to spend my life with you, why the hell would I want to make you feel bad?" I replied.

"I don't know, but please don't leave me. I'm so sorry for being a dick, yesterday."

We cuddled for a while, both quite hungover, and finally

started laughing about it all. He went downstairs for breakfast to join his parents, who were already up and cooking.

I called Polly, as I still felt vulnerable.

She said, "Love, it's all good, you're just getting a bit like the rest of us steady couples. We all argue about silly things."

I spoke to the kids before going downstairs to eat breakfast with Robert and his parents. I was feeling fragile and exhausted from trying to be perfect and, deep down, wasn't sure that Robert could handle a girl who wasn't.

We left later that day and, en route, we stopped for a coffee.

Robert turned around and said, "I'm really sorry, babe, for giving you a shit time. It wasn't my intention; I think we're both just stressed."

I agreed, as I had earlier, and said, "I love you, but I feel very tired. I just need you to understand that it's not you, it's that I'm working so much to try and keep my head above water."

He nodded, and we went back to the car. When we arrived at my house, he came in to say hello to Polly and the kids. We had agreed in the car that he would go to his place, as we both needed some space. I gave him a massive hug, hoping he understood that I wasn't rejecting him. He drove away, and I closed the door. Polly cracked open a bottle and we sat for some of the evening, talking about relationships. Chey had taken Rosie for a walk and gone to the pub with her. That was his dream; a woman by his side who didn't argue. Polly and I spoke about how men compared to women, and how differences can sabotage a relationship.

"I feel like it's okay for me to be his emotional punching bag," I said, "but when I need him to be mine, he becomes destructive, and somehow, it becomes about him, again."

Polly answered, "Love can be a weakness, and some people use it as a weapon in a relationship. Maybe Robert has his own issues that go deeper than you think."

"I can't be sure, but you're right, there's something volatile in the way he turns things around."

"Kat, you'll be fine. The man loves the pants off of you. You're just growing up together – it's normal to have these moments."

The weeks went on, and Robert started coming to my place more frequently, as money was still tight on my end, and I couldn't afford a babysitter. We decided to go to his parents' place, along with the kids, and have a long weekend away. Maria and Michael had made an extra bedroom for the kids, and we slept in a bedroom next to them. Our families were integrated, and it was lovely to be away. Maria and I always had such a good time. Joanie came over, too, and I loved being with these upfront, strong women while drinking wine. Meanwhile, the men watched sports, and the kids played. Maria was feisty, but gentle and kind at the same time. She was always supportive of me and was very open about how Robert had always been a bit of a loner. She said she was so happy that he'd met a strong woman like me. She adored the children, and Magnus and Pepper loved their new extended family. I learned that Maria was an adopted child and that, when her mother had died, she'd gone to look for her birth mother. Eventually, she'd found her, but her birth mum had said she had no interest in meeting her. It was a heart-breaking story, but it kind of explained why she'd gotten pregnant at such a young age.

Maria's story made her into a real person, with real problems and a real life, and as such, I knew she was able to relate to the life challenges of other people. We often had deep talks, late into the night. Robert was just happy to see me getting on with his family so well. I told her that I'd been so tired that, just a few days before, I'd suggested to the kids that we go to Richmond Park and walk Rosie. When we arrived, I realised I'd forgotten Rosie. The kids had found it amusing, and I had too, but really, my mind was overloaded. Similarly, I'd turned up to meetings on several occasions and actually forgotten the client's name.

"Kat, you're doing too much," she said, and I knew she was right. "It'll be easier when you and Robert live together. He can help you with the kids, and you'll not be on your own with the finances. Michael can build you a loft extension, and you'll both benefit from it."

I hugged and thanked her. Robert and I had our own challenges, but we were in love, and Maria was incredibly supportive. She didn't seem to care about her son being with a woman who already had two children. I suppose her life experiences had given her this liberal attitude.

"Life is what you make it, not how you plan it," she finished off.

After a great weekend, we carried on with work and life. It had been fifteen months since we started dating, and we were definitely getting into a rhythm. My parents invited us to Denmark and, I admit, I told Robert with some reluctance; part of me wanted to just be on my own, but he had just changed jobs and couldn't get the time off, anyway. I was still struggling to get enough money in, but my parents offered to pay for our tickets, and Robert said he'd look after Rosie. I was quite happy with the outcome. I was still feeling relieved that we'd managed to argue and overcome it, while at the same time accepting our differences. However, I still found it hard, after a hard day's work, to be that cuddly girlfriend. It was small stuff, but going to my parents' on my own was my idea of heaven. I loved the man so much, but I did need some space to breathe. I had been on my own for five years and was still getting used to someone wanting me around all the time. I couldn't even put him to bed at nine. It was slightly conflicting, as the loneliness I had felt was something I at times missed. I needed to find the balance, again.

Weeks before the kids and I left for Denmark, Robert and I booked a babysitter and went to 'Rock & Rose' to enjoy some 'us' time with his friends, Matthew and Gloria. They had been at the wedding too, and I had clicked quite well with Gloria. They lived nearby and had been married for six years. I arrived slightly late, as the babysitter was late, and they'd already started on the cocktails. When I walked in, Robert looked at me in a way that made me melt. He looked stunning in his suit jacket, jeans, and a white shirt. His hair was black and swirly, and his blue eyes fixed on mine – it was one of those moments where I couldn't imagine not waking up next to him and seeing those eyes for the rest of my life. We couldn't keep our hands off each other under the table, and we had to try not to be one of those annoying couples who are so besotted with each other that they might as well not be out with anyone else.

We had a beautiful dinner. Gloria and Matthew were the couple who I think everyone in Robert's circle wanted to be. They had a house in Teddington – she was a teacher, he was a broker, and they were happily married; it seemed easier for them than for a lot of the other couples, and it was a given that they were always going to be together. It was Matthew's second marriage, and his first one hadn't lasted long. Some couples just have this stamina; you know it's always going to be the two of them – it was exactly how I felt with Robert.

Gloria turned to me after a few Pornstar Martinis.

"Kat, Robert's last girlfriend was so boring. I love the fact that you're so independent and can challenge him."

"Thanks, babe, he really talks a lot about you and Matt, in such a good way."

"I haven't told anyone, yet, but Matt and I have been together now for six *long* years, and we're trying for a kid."

"I'm so happy for you, Gloria, but I don't blame you for waiting. As a teacher, you must have enough of kids when you're at work!"

"I wanted to ask you: when I have a kid, would you advise me to move to the countryside?"

"Definitely not, are you kidding me? You need a social network around you, you need to be able to call a friend who can jump in when you're about to duct tape your kids to their chairs and put them in front of the television."

"What else can you tell me?" she asked, laughing.

"You have to tell Matt to be kind when you take your clothes off, the first couple of months after giving birth – your body is all over the place, but it's important to be intimate again. I suppose just be the best you can be – it's a learning curve."

As the boys came over with a tray of shots, she nodded. It was going to be a long night. Matt asked Gloria what we'd been talking about and, after she revealed their new project to Robert, she hugged me and said, "Kat has given me great advice. Let's party!"

Robert looked at me in exactly the same way as when he'd first said he loved me, whispering gently in my ear, "I love you and everything you're about."

I smiled. I was so happy that all my worries floated away with his whisper.

When I finally went to Denmark, Robert texted me, but he was often so busy that he forgot to text me goodnight in the evening. I didn't dwell on it, as I knew he was into his new work position and doing well. Copenhagen was just like the old days – we stayed at my parents' beach house in Liseleje, and friends popped by (invited and uninvited) to see my mum, who was famous for her cooking. One day, my mum and I cooked all morning, knowing people would come by later that day. The sun was shining, and I was reminded in the best way that, when things were tough at home, the beach house in Denmark was a good place to visit.

My childhood friend, Christina, came by with her two kids, and when she arrived, I was shocked; she was about eight stone – all skin and bone – as her husband had left her. She'd found out her husband had been leading a double life for the previous eight years of the sixteen they'd been together. I remembered her wedding. She'd been dressed like a fairy princess (the result of her going to a Danish design college), and we'd all partied until five in the morning. She had been the last one to go to bed. I think she

even woke up in her wedding dress. She sat down, and our respec-
tive sets of kids ran out onto my mum and dad's lawn. Christina
started in straightaway.

"Fuck, Kat, I'm forty-one and wasted sixteen years on this
man. What the fuck do I do?"

Before I could answer, she was digging into my mum's food
and pouring herself a glass of wine.

"Babe, you have two beautiful kids, you know by now what
you want in bed, and younger men love a bit of MILF. Try to look
on the bright side."

"You know I'd enjoy that," she said, chewing, "but it's the
thought of doing it all again that exhausts me – the falling in love,
the compromises, the kids learning to like his kids, or whatever.
I'm exhausted by the thought of it."

I laughed but tried to explain to her that as soon as she found
the right man, she would find her way, just as I had with Robert. I
nodded as she spoke – it took hard work, hence why I was here
on my own.

The kids came running in, all sweaty and thirsty. Magnus
grabbed my mum's meatballs – we Danes call them 'frikadeller' –
and tucked in. Christina was still eating, so I poured drinks for
the kids. We were sitting under a sun roof, over a terrace
attached to my parent's house, looking out on the garden. We
heard a car drive into the driveway, and my friends Nicolai and
his wife, Charlotte, walked in. Nicolai had been a friend for
eighteen years, and we were like brother and sister. He'd also
brought his youngest kid. Charlotte had two other kids with
someone else, and Nicolai had taken them under his wing,
showing me that it could be done. My mum opened the door
and hugged Nicolai. They sat down, grabbed plates, and hovered
over the food, while my dad brought more drinks to the table.
Charlotte was, again, a very tall blonde woman with perfect legs
who looked stunning in whatever she wore, even after
three kids.

"How's London, Kat?" she asked. "When are we going to meet the new man?"

I responded, "Soon; I just came home to rest, for a bit. Business is tough, and I just feel a bit thin-skinned, if that makes sense."

"I get it," she said. "Your friend Nicolai here is like having another child, at the moment. He's been out a lot and pissed in our neighbour's window boxes the other night. I had to deal with an angry man who wanted me to buy new pelargoniums."

Nicolai, who is a typical Danish man, with his ash-blond hair, blue eyes, and great sense of style, was still chewing his food and mumbled, "It'll make them grow better, honey. I said that to you."

She raised her glass of wine.

"Well then, Nicolai, the only thing to do is to keep drinking. Then I can piss on your head, as you're getting a bit too bald for my liking."

We all burst out laughing. I wasn't sure how Nicolai felt, but that was Danish humour for you. It bounced around the room, and we all ate mum's food, as the kids played in the garden, occasionally dipping in for food and drinks. The garden was huge, with twenty tall birch and pine trees surrounding the edges, which was finished off with a fence. My dad had a small shed and a cherry tree next to it that we always picked from, when we could. My mum had bought loads of terracotta pots with hydrangeas, olive trees, and wild flower choices in them. It was a beautiful setting. We all agreed that it was nice to see Christina actually eat. We walked down to the beach and had a swim in the sea and, when we returned, we found that my mum had made cakes and set out a cheeseboard. We ate more, drank more, and Nicolai went for a snooze on a garden lounger. The wind was almost still, the bees were buzzing around the cherry tree, the kids were playing croquet, and we girls sat around with my parents, trying to work out men. I said that, if we cracked the man-whisperer idea, we could all be made for life after writing a book about it.

The girls shook their heads, and Christina said, "I'm actually not sure if I want to know everything men like. I think it could put me off them forever."

We laughed and carried on trying to solve the mystery of testosterone. It was so warm, for April. By the end of the day, I felt warm, tired, and happy. Christina had a beach house around the corner, and we agreed to meet at the beach the next day, even though the thought of me standing next to her eight-stone frame wasn't appealing.

The kids and I put on our pyjamas and curled up on the couch to watch a movie, and my father turned the wood stove on. I tried to get ahold of Robert, but he texted me saying that he was out with the boys. I sent him a kiss goodnight, and he told me he loved me.

The next day, we woke up so refreshed that I felt like a different person. I checked my emails and found that work was under control. We had breakfast. The kids were already getting that rested feeling of not having the pressures of school and homework. It was all getting so much better. I still felt slightly stressed, but my parents reassured me, saying they'd continue to support me financially, if I needed it. It was embarrassing to ask at the age of thirty-nine. I did have Robert to support me, but not financially. Or, at least, I had him when he wasn't stressed himself.

After breakfast, we put on our beach clothes and went down to meet Christina and her kids. My mum had made us a picnic basket, and my guess was that Christina and her kids would be eating the most.

It was time to get back, and Robert said he'd meet us at the airport. It was always sad to say goodbye to my parents, as it meant I was going back to the reality of money worries, tight schedules, and single motherhood. This time, it was different –

my parents had offered some help and, more importantly, I had Robert. I couldn't wait for his hug.

We arrived in Heathrow, but Robert was running late. I had some beautiful whiskey I'd bought for him, and I was excited to smell his skin and sleep next to him again. He came running into view, visibly flustered. He hugged me but, straightaway, I knew something was wrong. The kids were excited to see him, and we went back home. He hugged me and kissed me, but he seemed down, and I suddenly felt he was on a different planet. When I tried asking him, he avoided talking about himself. My first thought was that he was depressed about work and other things. We went to bed early but didn't make love. He barely touched me, and I knew deep inside what was happening.

The next morning, he kissed me and hurried out to work. I asked him via text if we should still go to his place and mentioned that the babysitter was booked for the night, so we could have some alone time. I took the kids to school and, on my way back, my phone beeped. There it was: 'Shall we meet at the pub first and just have a drink?' I knew then that this was 'the talk' – the end. My faith crumbled; I knew that things weren't going to end well for me, and I started shaking. I texted back, 'If you're breaking up with me, it would be good to know now. I don't want to be hanging around all day, not knowing if I'm dumped or not.'

He responded, 'I'm sorry, I can't do it.'

Was that it? I'd been dumped by the love of my life by text. I called back, and he picked up and immediately started talking in a panicked tone, saying, "I can't do it, I can't do the stepdad thing, I can't pretend I want to see your kids grow up into teenagers. I'm suffocated, and I can't do it."

I felt everything leaving me. Never had anyone taken so much out of me as in that moment. I felt heartache creeping back into my body.

I was angry and said, "You promised me you were never going

to leave me, you promised me a life together, you said you loved me!"

"I do love you, I love you more than anything, but I'm not even sure I want kids, and I feel like I should be loving Magnus and Pepper, but I'm not sure if I can; not like you want me to."

I boiled over. He'd dumped me and used my kids as an excuse. He hadn't been led into this relationship blindfolded; he had *wanted* to meet the kids. I was devastated.

"Robert, you can fuck off. If you loved me, you'd love the fact that I am who I am, and that includes being a mum. You're a panicked, insecure, pathetic boy who I hope never finds love. Get your stuff in an hour, and make sure you're quick; I can't get you out of my life quickly enough. I won't be here to look at your ugly face and soul. You're a fraudster, and you're definitely not the man I thought you were. I mean, who the fuck tells a mum who fought for her kids that you're not sure you can love them? That's the best way to get rid of me, well done. I never asked you to love them – all I asked was for you to be their friend."

Hanging up, I realised I'd been screaming down the phone, and said some unforgivable things. My throat was sore. I frantically started packing all his stuff – his socks, his underwear, his clothes, suits, gifts that he'd given me – all in a pile on the floor. I dumped his bicycle on top of the pile, smashed all his whiskey glasses, and took Rosie to the park. I called Kirsten, and suddenly the anger faded, and I just collapsed on the grass. I started almost howling, sobbing, screaming. Nothing I shouted down the phone made any sense. How could I have been so wrong about the man I loved, again? She knew and just listened. She was in shock, as we'd all thought this was it. Rosie sat next to me. I couldn't handle the pain – it felt like I was dying. I kept screaming, finally stumbling out words that made sense.

"I can't do this, Kirsten, I can't do this again. I don't have enough in me to fight this, and I can't surrender. This will eat me alive. I don't know what to say to the kids – I feel like I'm losing my mind."

She replied, "I know it looks black and cold right now, and that it's an insanely scary place to be, but I've walked there before you, and I know there's a way out, even though you can't find it, right now. These are not empty words; do you hear me? There's a way out. Let the bricks fall – we'll build you up again from much stronger stuff. When life blows a hole in your soul, Kat, it's time to build an extension! For now, feel the pain, but don't fear it. It's there to release, not to trap. Hang in there."

I put the phone down, and I embraced every emotion that came into my body. I buried my face in Rosie's fur and kept sobbing. After an hour, I went back to the house and found that Robert had taken his stuff. The presents that he'd given me had been left behind. I broke down again, and was crying when my phone rang. It was Iris, asking me out for a coffee.

"You okay? You sound weird," she said.

"He's left me, Iris. He's broken me, and I don't know what to do."

"I'll be there in a minute," she said. She'd only known me for a few years, as a mum from school, but she was willing to drop everything to come to my rescue. She was at my house within ten minutes and had brought a bottle of wine with her. She poured a glass for me and I just cried in her arms, trying to explain to her what had happened.

She just kept saying, "How the fuck did this happen? He loves you, he's crazy for you. Why did he do this? Do you think he'll come back?"

It carried on like that as I sobbed and drank wine in the middle of the afternoon, looking at the stuff he'd left behind. Iris called Robyn, the other mum from school, who also came over. They both hugged me and listened to my howling and kept giving me tissues. The afternoon wore on, and I knew the kids had to be picked up. My face was swollen and sore, and I looked like a watermelon. Iris went to school to pick up the kids. She and Robyn agreed that I shouldn't be left alone and called Kirsten, who came around to give me a Valium.

"It will make you calm and take the first few days off of what might feel a bit like a daze," she said "and no, they're not so strong that a fire won't wake you up."

She called Polly, who joined us, and they all looked at me with sad eyes. I just wanted to run away. I didn't want those sad eyes to look at me again. He'd promised this was never going to happen. Now, I had to find a way to tell the children that Robert wasn't coming back. *Is he even going to say goodbye to the kids? Should I allow him to?* I knew this was the end. Hate was a mild word for how I felt inside. I'd again been betrayed and fooled. I wondered if he'd decided to leave me during a trip to Hastings, at the sight of my arse when I'd been squatting to pee. Or was it when I'd sneakily farted, thinking he was asleep? Nothing made sense anymore, and I was clinging to explanations to escape the fact that the man was a weak creature and couldn't do it. I had again fallen for someone who wanted the fantasy, the cloud nine feeling, the rush. That wasn't reality, though, and I had again allowed myself to be with someone who seemed unable to cope with the simple facts of life. I looked in the mirror and was sorry for what I saw.

When Iris arrived with the children, I told them that Mummy was upset because Robert had been stationed to China for work. I couldn't have wished him further away, and it seemed the right thing to say, at that moment. The wine had something to do with my judgement. Magnus looked at me with his brown eyes, and sadness came over his face.

"Did he not want to say goodbye to us?"

There it was, the guilt of bringing this man into their lives, making them believe he cared. I explained to my kids that it was the adults' fault, and I just needed some time to adjust. I told them we could always see if there was a chance Robert would be allowed back from China. I ordered takeaway, opened another bottle of wine, and my sisterhood came together. More friends dropped in and, by eleven, I was tucked up in bed. The kids were fast asleep and felt loved after having all the mums, and their kids, in our house. I took my computer and deleted all the Facebook friends I'd met through Robert: Gloria, Matthew, Dave, Zoe, and more. I then took my phone and deleted his mobile number and his family's numbers. It was liberating and sad, and I knew it was the only thing I could do.

After a few hours, I got up, went into the kids' bedroom, and said, "I'm so sorry, guys, for letting you down."

I kissed them and fell asleep, crying. My heart was broken, but my mind was still. The only thing I had to do was get up the next day and move forward.

I woke up very early and had ten seconds before I remembered that Robert was gone. I sobbed into my pillow, because I didn't want to wake the kids up. My heart was physically aching. My chest hurt and, while I was getting up, I wondered whether the doctor would have any medicine for a broken heart. I kept my strong face on around the kids, but I could tell they knew. *I feel so guilty.*

I made them breakfast, packed lunch, helped Pepper with her hair, and brought them to school. My kids didn't owe me anything, and I wanted to protect them as much as I could from this mess. My friends were texting me constantly to see if I was okay, but every time my phone went off, I hoped it was Robert. Days went by in a daze. I couldn't bring myself to call my parents, and I couldn't do any work. Instead, I sat around watching episodes of *Sex and the City*.

Robert texted me once and asked me if I was okay. I replied, 'no I am not', and all he replied was, 'I'm sorry'. There was nothing he could say to make me feel better. He'd chosen not to have me in his life, and he'd never spoken to me about wanting to leave. I felt hopeless.

A week later, I still felt raw. I went for a meeting at Kew

Gardens with a big client who was organising a three-hundred-guest event. She was amazing, and the last time I'd seen her was when I'd been with Robert and planning my own future and possible wedding.

I met her at the venue, and she asked, "How is everything, Kat? I can't wait to hear about your new ideas for the wedding, isn't it great to be in love?"

My chin began shaking and I said, "Oh my god, yes, I love it, let's sit down and talk about your wedding."

I couldn't mix my professional and personal lives – it was too painful, especially when I'd just thrown out my own book of wedding ideas. I reminded myself that I'd gotten rid of a man who'd given me a pan after our first argument, as an apology, and who saw a rugby game as a romantic weekend away, but as much as I tried to bring up all his negatives, I was in agony. All I wanted was to scream. I realised that, with Casper and having the kids, I'd lost my identity and found my way back. Now, with Robert, I'd had my heart broken, and I had no idea how to repair it.

Wine and Snot Bubbles

❦

I'd been abandoned by the man I'd chosen to introduce to my children. I knew that this wasn't my mess, it was his. I had to let him go, as he wasn't ready for me. It was my mess that I'd introduced him and his whole family to the kids. That, I had to deal with.

It dawned on me that he'd only once been honest with me about his doubts. He'd mentioned that he found it hard to find his role within my family unit, and I'd told him that I didn't expect him to be a stepfather. I didn't even expect him to be financially or emotionally involved. We'd concluded that it was something we'd both have to work at. Magnus and Pepper had a father – not a great one, but he was alive. Besides, their grandparents had really made all the difference, so I asked only for Robert to be their friend. We both knew that this needed some kind of dedication and compromise from him, and maybe Robert never had this in him. Only he knew.

In the weeks after the breakup, I took half a sleeping tablet each night, as I simply couldn't sleep. It gave me the strength to get through to the next day. I had such dry eyes from crying that I scratched my eyelid with a kitchen towel. I went to the bathroom and put some cream on my cut eyelid and felt a terrible burn. I looked at the tube and realised I had put Magnus's wart cream in my eye. I screamed and called Iris, who watched the kids while I took a cab to A&E. I sat until one in the morning, and the nurse flushed my eye out with salt water, which burned even worse. I was given more cream and a clap on the shoulder. The doctor told me I was lucky not to have damaged my eye. I got home, and Iris didn't know whether to scream or laugh when she saw me – half of my face was swollen, and my eye wasn't able to open. I thanked her so much for looking after the kids, hugged her, and took half a Valium before going to bed. I couldn't even cry – I was simply too tired. My thoughts drifted to Robert, and I wondered what he was doing. I decided that pragmatism was a huge part of parenthood and acknowledged that 'finding the one' was difficult because it was based on being emotional, rather than practical. So many single mums I've met settled for any man who loved them for who they were.

As one friend put it, "He smiles in the morning, he says he loves me, he's great with the children, and he's accommodating in bed. The rest, I can do myself, so why wouldn't I choose him to be the one? I might not be overly in love with him, but it's hard out there, and I'm holding on to this one!"

Robyn had said to me, "A lot of the real fathers don't even know how to deal with their kids, so how can we single mums expect to find a boyfriend who'll do the right thing? It's unreasonable to ask him to. Put it this way," she said, "the last time I got drunk with the family, I put my shoes on the wrong way around and sat with a bucket in my lap, all the way home in the car, while the kids took photos of me because their dad thought it was funny. I mean, yes, I was too drunk, but I hadn't eaten enough, that day. Later on, I saw his phone, and he'd set one of the pictures as his wallpaper. I mean, for fuck's sake."

I'd laughed, but my thoughts had gone back to what she'd said about me asking for too much. I thought it was unreasonable of

Robert to let me think he could do it. He'd been happy until recently; I hadn't laid any pressure on him, he'd put all the pressure on himself. He'd thought that this was what was expected of him, regardless of the actual expectations I'd communicated, and he'd made his mind up without consulting me, discussing his fears, or even giving me, or the relationship, another chance. He had panicked. I was in the same place as I'd been before.

I suppose all the conversations with the girls helped me rethink who I was and who I was looking to share my life with. Did I want the man who would be an emotional rollercoaster and a big risk, or did I want to take the safe route, with a man who had the same qualities as my friend's new husband? What did I want? Was there a real man out there? I knew in the soppiest way that what I wanted was to say, "I love you," to someone and to really feel it, and hear it back too. I wanted what I'd had with Robert.

Being *in* love is so different to love. Love is commitment, and involves years of sacrifice and compromise to make it work. Being in love is arousing and addictive, but it won't last unless you're willing to put the hard work in. We all know this, deep inside, so why did it take me by surprise every freaking time? Being in love is a beautiful feeling, and I wish sometimes it was sustainable, but it's not reality. The reality is that you have to work hard on getting back in love with someone who leaves old coffee cups everywhere, dirty pants on the floor, and his pubic hair on the edge of the bathtub. Love means dealing with someone who squeezes the toothpaste from the middle, and that occasional moment pretending you're enjoying it in bed when you'd actually rather have the extra twenty minutes sleep. Love is dedication to making it work.

My single motherhood had become my grounded place, the place for the men I met to feel safe. I think my maternal nature suited the men I saw – I was so used to the role that it extended into my relationships too. The problem is, you don't fuck your mother. I fell asleep still arguing with myself. I had to take responsibility in this too.

Partway through one of my biggest heartbreaks ever, I spoke to Sam, who had become one of my more hapless and inattentive friends. She said, "Why don't you forget about him, now? It's been a month, and you're wasting too much time on him."

I wondered how someone could become so cold.

I gently asked, "Oh, do you know where the off button is?"

It was her reality, and she hadn't been trying to be cruel, but her thoughtlessness made me realise that we had grown apart. She couldn't comprehend what I was going through and just wanted to fix me, so she could feel adequate as a friend.

I said, "Sam, listen to my feelings and less to the details of how the relationship occurred, lasted, and died. Don't try to make too much sense of his actions, but just listen, understand why I'm sad. I just need a hug and someone to listen."

"Right," she said, "I'm going to the hairdresser, now, can I call you after? And don't forget: you're a stunning girl, it'll be no problem finding another one. Bye!"

I knew it was the beginning of the end for our friendship. I sat for a moment before remembering that I did have friends who understood. I found my iPod and put on Billy Joel's *She's Always a Woman to Me*. I knew Sam wouldn't ring back, and I learned to love some of my friends with a distance.

I used the time after Robert to learn about myself. The fact that I'd been lulling him into my mother's sphere was a revelation for me. When I didn't have the energy to give him anything apart from grief, he didn't understand that I had needs – sometimes, he would have to stroke my hair and be strong for me, as I was for him. I couldn't be the strong one all of the time. I had to take responsibility for this; I had been so independent, strong, and powerful that when I started halting and needed him to step up, he didn't know how. I had made myself the alpha male in the relationship, the one who could cope with anything while taking care of others, which in reality I couldn't, and he had allowed it to happen.

The days went by, and I still missed him terribly. I daydreamed about him approaching me and wanting me back and saying what a huge mistake he'd made. I'd tell him about my epiphany, and we'd learn from it and live happily ever after. Realising this wasn't going to happen, one evening, after the kids had gone to bed, I sat browsing through my files on the computer. I had the empty feeling of everything being pointless – I was just being chased constantly by this loneliness, and spent my days looking for anything that could fill the hole.

I came across a file where I'd written down my thoughts, as the therapist had suggested. I started reading. It was all about the turmoil of the court case, Casper, and losing the shop, and I read the thoughts of someone who was angry, hurt, and mistreated. I wanted to turn this person's identity around. I didn't want to be the one everyone felt sorry for. I wanted to be happy and strong and grateful for what was in front of me. I wanted single mothers to understand that it's a fucker to be on their own, after meeting men who leave as soon as the shit hits the fan, and I wanted to enjoy being single again before I even thought about committing to another man. Self-pity and trying to avoid loneliness wasn't the solution. I picked the file out and started writing about being a single mum, and the pictures floated in front of me, like a movie. I was buzzing, as I suddenly realised I was here, at this moment, at this stage, because I was meant to write this book. This was my own process – I was slowly finding out who I was and what made me happy, and no man was involved. I wrote until two in the morning and collapsed with my laptop on my bed. I woke up with Magnus pulling at my arm, telling me that we'd overslept, and I realised I hadn't even had a Valium or a glass of wine. I'd slept better than I had in weeks. I got out of bed and told the kids it didn't matter because we weren't going to go to school.

"Are you going to cry, Mum?" asked Magnus. He was used to me changing plans when I was upset.

"No, Magnus, I'm actually really happy. I'm going to write a book for other single mummies, so they know that they're not alone."

Both Pepper and Magnus looked at me, confused, and I sat them down and, taking care to be as present as I could, I looked into their small and beautiful morning faces, breathed in, and started talking.

"When Mummy makes choices, I understand that you just have to follow, and I also know that you don't get much say because of your age, but I want you to make the right choices when you grow up, and it's my job to guide you along the way."

Pepper yawned and scratched her bird's nest of hair, looking even more confused. Magnus, on the other hand, looked at me with his hazel eyes and grabbed my hand with his beautiful olive skin.

"Yes, Mum, continue."

"Well, if I am to guide you, then I need to know what path I'm on myself, and figure out what makes me happy."

Pepper said, "I want to go to New York, Mum. That would make me happy."

Magnus shushed her. "Let Mum speak, for god's sake."

He was taking his role as the man of the house very seriously, for an eight-year-old.

"I want to be a success as a mother, as a human being, as a writer, as a daughter, and I want to inspire single mummies to be driven by the same things. If I can write a book, then Mummy will have made something successful already because I'll have finished something I always wanted to do, and everything else that comes after will be a bonus, kiddos. You see?"

I sat in the bed with my arms in the air, as if they were wings flapping away. I didn't want them to only feel failure and to feel like they were missing something. I wanted to share my stories, trials, heartbreaks, and happy stories so they could understand and focus on finding out for themselves what made them happy.

The kids were looking very confused and Magnus said, "So, Mum, are we not going to school because you're writing a book today?"

I answered, "No; you're not going to school today because we need a family day. The best way I can explain it is that Mummy lost her compass, a while back, but now I've found it again. I think we should celebrate it later and go to the cinema and Pizza Express."

The kids jumped up, and we all jumped on the bed. The kids looked at me, still slightly confused, but they were happy. They were off school! They went back to bed to play on their tablets, and I called school to tell them that the kids had tummy viruses. I went back to writing my book. It was the beginning of a transition, I knew it.

While I was working, writing, and trying not to call Robert in moments of, *I know he loves me, I just need to reach out,* I wondered if he knew how much I'd loved him. I found I was rolling into my previous role of being emotionally unavailable. I had to fix my broken heart, and I simply didn't know how. I'd thought I was going to marry Robert, believing he accepted me as I was, to have his child and build a future together. I was thirty-nine years old, and I was realising that maybe I wasn't going to have another child. The faith that a man would want me as a full-time partner, with two kids in tow, felt impossible, and I was mourning more than just my broken heart and my kid's disappointment. I was thinking that I'd have to prepare myself to be on my own until the kids had grown up, which meant no more children.

It was an important time, and I filled it by making great new friendships, cementing several old ones, and learning that many of my old friends couldn't deal with another disaster in my life. I accepted it and emotionally got rid of them. I felt that even though I had a great history with some of my old friends, it didn't mean I was supposed to be great friends with them forever. We all change depending on what life throws at us. In certain phases of life, you realise that you don't have anything in common anymore, and you're presented with a natural pause in the friendship. The pause can be pressed and made to resume but, after so many pauses, sometimes it's better to just stop.

I called Kirsten on a bad night.

"I can't write; I'm too sad. It's hopeless − I think I've got writer's block, which is awesome, as I've never been a writer before. I'm hopeless!"

"You're not hopeless, the men in your life are. You're heartbroken and going through the pain. It will go Kat, it will go. I promise you this. You'll get through this and above it. You're not alone − we're here for you and refuse to let you go through this on your own. I'll be at yours tomorrow, at six, with food for you and the kids."

I kept working, but I didn't write for a year.

Robert never gave me an opportunity to reflect on what had happened. After the one text where I dismissed him, he never once got back to me, so it took me a long time to find closure. I reached out a few times, but he didn't respond. When I started writing again it helped, and eventually, I found my own closure, but it was hard and very confusing. I used it as a part of my transition to finishing this book. It was the only thing that truly made me happy, apart from my kids and Rosie.

When he left, I realised that lots of my grief was for the future that I'd wanted − that he'd taken away with him. With Casper, I'd been sad to lose the family unit I always thought I was going to have; it was never him I grieved. Seeing families walking in the park or in restaurants always gave me a slight ache in the heart, until I came to terms with it and loved what we had, me and the kids. I learned to look ahead, not back. I had to do the same with Robert. My lesson with Robert was that I wasn't ready, either.

If not him, it would have to be someone else. I lost my focus and couldn't see how I could have such a connection with someone else, but I might, I might not – I'm happy to leave it open and see what happens. It's nice to be excited about the future, again – for too long, I mourned the past. I felt like a fish out of water, but now I've made it back into the sea. I knew I couldn't force my feelings aside and just suddenly skip down the road with a big smile, but I decided to work on being present. I would enjoy what was in front of me. It was yet another lesson learned from heartbreak. *Take small steps.*

The thought of opening up to a man again was scary, but it wasn't something I had to deal with right away. I started feeling better when Petra reminded me that moaning and hating your life isn't going to make the good stuff happen.

My months were up and down, but I was getting much lighter in my mind set. I did have a bad week where I crashed after seeing Robert passing through Richmond – I thought I was never going to get better. I was crying so much that Iris, Kirsten, Robyn, and Polly had to make me and the kids food, rock me in bed, and keep telling me everything was going to be okay. We'd have lived on takeaway paid for on credit cards, and me curled up on the couch, otherwise. One day, I came back from several meetings with happy clients getting married to find fresh bread and a candle at my door, and a note from Iris saying she loved me. Polly sat with me until one in the morning and just listened to the same record playing, "Why? Why? Why?" I got through it because of them: the sisterhood. They made me feel they would move mountains for me, and it made me feel less alone.

The fact that Robert and I lived in the same area wasn't ideal, and I avoided Richmond a lot. Kingston became my new crib, but it wasn't as romantic to shop and walk in. I cursed him for taking Richmond from me, as well. Maria and Joanie sent me a text saying they loved me and were devastated. They were full of integrity, and we left it at that. They felt just as much mourning as I did, but we agreed it was best not to be in contact. Robert hadn't communicated with them, either. He had apparently thrown himself into his work and had refused to talk about me. I knew it was his guilt with regards to the children, but I had no sympathy for him. They kept asking for him, and I kept saying his boss had kept him in Beijing. He never offered to say goodbye to the children, and I lost a huge amount of respect for him. It felt so undignified.

I got invited to go on a boat with Kirsten and the kids. We went up and down the river in Richmond. It was one of those days where I had no makeup on and looked tired. I wore old, ripped jeans, a cap, and trainers. I had hit the phase of not giving much thought to what I looked like – who would give a shit, anyway? These thoughts came through me daily, with regards to men. The kids were trying to steer the boat and were enjoying the tranquillity of the water as it splashed them gently. We lay at the front of the boat, enjoying the sun, and Kirsten introduced the kids to the 'Captain's wee', which involved sticking your arse over the railing and weeing in the river. As there were a lot of people out and the sun was beaming, we decided to stop at one of the pubs along the river in the town centre to use the toilets. As we left, I spotted Robert and all his mates. I had partied and dined with all of them in the past.

"Go ahead," I said to the kids, who still thought he was in China. I stood for a minute, wondering if I should say hello to them. I walked towards them and said, "Hi, you guys okay?"

I gave them all a hug before remembering I hadn't used deodorant that day. It was the ultimate 'I am ugly and stink' moment. Robert looked at me and smiled, giving me a hug.

"You alright?" he asked. He looked amazing. White shirt, wavey black hair, and beautiful eyes. I started babbling away, my legs like jelly. I was speaking about nothing in a long burst of verbal diarrhoea. I finally stopped when Kirsten started waving, her eyes telling me I should stop making an arse of myself. I said my goodbyes and walked towards the boat. *Why didn't I wear my fucking tight jeans?*

"How did it go?" she asked.

"Well, it could have gone a lot better," I replied.

She looked at me with a frown.

"I know what we need," she said, and ran down into her cabin. She emerged with a bottle of prosecco and two plastic cups. "Kat, you don't want to keep looking back. You need to live now. He wanted his freedom, now he's got it. Men like that will always look for more than what's in front of them. It's become intolerable, with how many boxes we women have to tick before we're good enough. In the old days, it was just about pure love."

I couldn't agree more with her. She started pouring out the prosecco. The kids slowly steered the boat along the river, with Kirsten's help. They hadn't seen Robert, and I was grateful to the universe for that. I sneakily looked over my shoulder, knowing he was looking. I felt the ache around my heart and took a sip. However ridiculous it sounded, I simply knew that he would be ready one day, but I also knew I would be in a different place. I had wanted him to love me just the way I was, and he had shown me he couldn't. The bubbles on my tongue were blissful. Deep inside, I celebrated that I had been strong enough to approach him and his friends. I knew we were over and that Kirsten was right. He had his freedom. I was on a journey to make myself complete, regardless of who was in my life. It was a transition.

I shed a tear and Kirsten said, "Seriously, girl, you're the one with balls, here, and I actually think you might have some of theirs hanging around your neck too. Be proud. Don't cry, my love."

After a while, I felt a powerful feeling coming from somewhere deep inside of me. It was pride at how strong I really was. I felt an urge to write and wondered if I should start that same evening.

"Mum," Magnus said, "can we bring Rosie, next time, so the whole family is here on the boat?"

"Yeah," Pepper shouted. "Rosie is family, we need to show her this, she'd love it!"

I looked at their smiling faces. They were truly happy. Kirsten gave me a hug and took the steering wheel, the sun shining overhead. The kids sat next to me on either side, and we enjoyed the breeze the slow ride gave us.

"Maybe she can come on the boat with us, but let's enjoy it now and look forward to telling her all about it, okay?" I said.

I could feel my heart softening. The sound of water was tranquillising, and by just listening to their voices and sitting here, not feeling alone, I was in bliss. The kids nodded, and we fell into a nice silence, watching the sky, as we drifted down the river. The bubbles kept going, and we started sailing home. We were a happy, strong family, and we had some amazing friends to share the view with.

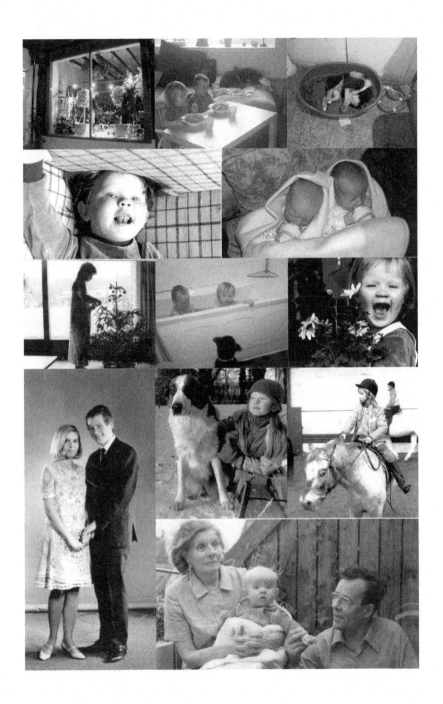

About the Author

Katja Berg is a Danish entrepreneur, author, and single mother. She was born in Frederiksberg, Copenhagen and moved to London at the age of eighteen.

She now lives In Richmond upon Thames in South West London with her twins.

She owns two successful businesses, one as a floral designer for fashion legends such as Vivienne Westwood and wedding venues such as Kew Gardens, as well as boutique hotels in Surrey and central London.

Her other business is a styling company called Bergdorf & Green focusing on venues, caterers, wedding dress makers, and much more in the wedding industry.

Her first book *A Rubber Face with a Stripper's Name* is based on the story of her life.

It is the story of the struggles faced by single mums. It is about sisterhood, relationships, and finding yourself.

Through her writing, Katja hopes to inspire and connect with other women who have been through, or are going through, similar experiences.

If you feel inspired to reach out, you can get in touch with Katja here.

https://www.katjaberg.com

Acknowledgments

Writing this book has been the most scary, thrilling, deflating, and exciting rollercoaster journey of my life. My mood would shift from excitement to utter frustration in a beat. Some days, I would wake up at 4 a.m., scrunch my yellow post-it notes in a ball, and shuffle to my desk to start writing. It was the only quiet time I had. No kids, no work, no dog. Just me and my thoughts. But as Maya Angelou (one of my favourite poets) said:

"There is no greater agony than bearing an untold story inside of you."

You often hear that writing a book is like having a baby. Well I have twins, and I can only agree. My friend, beautiful Sisse, kept telling me to push, push, and push some more whenever I was about to back out and throw my computer out of the window. "Don't let it get stuck in your birth canal," she would say. Sisse was so right.

There were those fretful days where I told myself that I was no author. No, not me. Authors have degrees in creative writing, and study the art of writing for years. But my beautiful friends would say, "Who says? Is it not writing a book and putting it out there that makes you one? Are we not all one when we write our diaries?" They were right, of course, and I encourage anyone who has an 'itch' to do the same. Don't let fear rule what you are going to do next in life. I had to tell myself this many times. After all, I was the woman who invited three-hundred clients to a Christmas advent party I was hosting, and I wrote that I would be serving 'malt wine' as opposed to 'mulled wine' on the invitation. People still came to my party, with a grin on their faces, I admit.

In my search for editing and publishing guidance, and for someone to help me tone down my jarring swear words (I do swear a lot), I found Bronwyn Hemus from Standout Books. I sent her my manuscript of 92,000 words and she slashed off 30,000 words in the first round of editing. She wrote me a report explaining the craft of writing and helped me understand how a reader would see the story. I cried for three days and sent her an angry email explaining that English was not my first language and that I was never a strong academic in school, but I had a story to tell and I wanted her to acknowledge it. She called me and comforted me, and said that editing was a brutal process, and welcomed me to the world of writing. I told her that she may as well have called my newborn an ugly baby, and she acknowledged that it was hard for me. She called me an author. Me, an author! Coming from her, I believed it and suddenly I started believing in myself and my story. Trusting myself and the editing process helped me become a better writer.

My relationship with Bronwyn was the beginning of a very long journey punctuated with many sleepless nights, and even more scribbles and post-it notes. Without her, it would not have happened. Bronwyn got me. She dove deep into my story and she helped me understand every word, sentence, and chapter. She was not afraid of making herself unpopular with me because she wanted to help me get the message out in the best way possible. Thank you, Bronwyn.

Her husband Alex, co-owner of Standout Books, has on many occasions, I am sure, wanted to jump off a bridge after talking to me. Alex has built my website, helped me design my book cover, and has taken care of all the marketing of this book. I once sent him fourteen emails in one day, and they were all about the colour of the petals on my cover. Bless him! Thank you, Alex.

Thank you Penny, for you know, just about everything. I love you.

When I have felt scared about publishing this book, and the way people would judge me, my sisterhood have been there to support me. They reminded me that writing this book is a success in itself and anything else is a bonus. Girls, I have succeeded in something I have always wanted to do. Yay, I did it!

We single mums are needy creatures, and we need that little bit extra from our friends. It's tough as everyone is so busy. I get it, but I want us all to be more considerate. I apologise now to all my gorgeous friends for being the one who has always asked for a little extra. I love you all so much.

Single mums have to (need to) evolve in a completely different way when a break up happens, so I want to tell my friends and their husbands or partners that this story isn't about you or your relationships. It's about me and how becoming a single parent can create a distance between people with partners and people without. It is something we deal with every day.

This story is about being a single Danish mum and the conversations I've had with my soul. It is a painful one to tell, but it is also full of hope. This book is for all the single mums out there surviving from one day to the next. You are not alone and you can do this.

Lightning Source UK Ltd.
Milton Keynes UK
UKOW04f2135031017
310315UK00001B/10/P